MW01123314

NETT.

Begonia Culture for Amateurs.

Gardeners' Library.

Book of Gardening: A Handbook of Horticulture. Very fully Illustrated. 1 *vol., demy 8vo, cloth gilt, about* 1,200 *pp., price* 16/- *nett, by post,* 16/8.

Popular Bulb Culture. A Practical and Handy Guide. Fully Illustrated. *Price* 1/- *nett, by post* 1/2.

Carnation Culture for Amateurs. Illustrated. *Price* 1/- *nett, by post,* 1/2.

Choice Ferns for Amateurs. Abridged from "The Book of Choice Ferns." Numerous Illustrations. *In cloth, price* 3/6 *nett, by post* 3/9.

Fruit Culture for Amateurs. With Chapters on Insect and other Fruit Pests by W. D. DRURY. Illustrated. *In cloth gilt, price* 3/6 *nett, by post* 3/10

Mushroom Culture for Amateurs. Revised and with New Illustrations. *Price* 1/- *nett, by post,* 1/2.

Tomato Culture for Amateurs. A Practical Manual. Illustrated. *Price* 1/- *nett, by post* 1/2.

Vegetable Culture for Amateurs. Illustrated. *Price* 1/- *nett, by post,* 1/2.

Home Gardening. A Manual for the Amateur. Illustrated. *Price* 1/- *nett, by post* 1/2.

Cactus Culture for Amateurs. With Full and Practical Instructions for their Successful Cultivation. Profusely Illustrated. *In cloth gilt price* 5/- *nett, by post* 5/4.

Alpine Plants. With Illustrations from photographs by CLARENCE ELLIOTT. *In cloth, price* 3/6 *nett, by post* 3/9.

Orchids: Their Culture and Management. Beautifully Illustrated with 180 Engravings and 20 Coloured Plates. *In demy 8vo, cloth gilt extra, price* 25/- *nett, by post* 25/6.

Greenhouse Construction and Heating. With Instructions for Fixing the Same. Illustrated. *In cloth gilt, price* 3/6 *nett, by post* 3/9.

Greenhouse Management for Amateurs. Revised and Enlarged. Magnificently Illustrated. *In cloth gilt, price* 5/- *nett, by post* 5/4.

Chrysanthemum Culture. Illustrated. *Price* 1/- *nett, by post* 1/2.

Grape Growing for Amateurs. Illustrated. *Price* 1/- *nett, by post* 1/2.

Hardy Perennials and Old-fashioned Garden Flowers. Profusely Illustrated. *In cloth gilt, price* 3/6 *nett, by post* 3/10.

Roses for Amateurs. With Sixteen Plates. *Price* 1/- *nett, by post,* 1/2.

Open-Air Gardening. Beautifully Illustrated. *In demy 8vo, cloth gilt, price* 6/- *nett, by post,* 6/5.

LONDON: L. UPCOTT GILL, Bazaar Buildings, Drury Lane, W.C

Tuberous-Rooted Single Begonias.

(For this Illustration we are indebted to Messrs. Webb & Son, Wordsley, Stourbridge.)

BEGONIA CULTURE

FOR AMATEURS:

CONTAINING

FULL DIRECTIONS FOR THE SUCCESSFUL CULTI-
VATION OF THE BEGONIA, UNDER GLASS,
AND IN THE OPEN AIR.

———

ILLUSTRATED.

———

By B. C. RAVENSCROFT,

*Author of "Chrysanthemum Culture for Amateurs," "Tomato
Culture for Amateurs," &c., &c.*

THIRD EDITION

LONDON:
L. UPCOTT GILL, BAZAAR BUILDINGS, DRURY LANE, W.C.

NEW YORK:
CHARLES SCRIBNER'S SONS, 153-157, FIFTH AVENUE.

PREFACE.

THE Begonia has always been my favourite flower,
and I have so many times been asked for a short treatise
or pamphlet on its culture that I have at last put the
result of my fifteen years' experience into book form,
and trust that it will be read with equal pleasure and
profit by the innumerable growers of this charming plant
all over the country. The tuberous Begonia, as represented by the modern varieties, is not only an exquisitely
beautiful and showy flower, but is also by no means
difficult of management; yet, owing to the want of a little
practical experience, failures, especially in raising the
plants from seed, are very numerous. I hope and believe
that the present little treatise may be the means of
preventing many of such losses in the future, and of
rendering the culture of the plant even more general
and successful than it is at the present time.

B. C. RAVENSCROFT.

CHAPTER I.

INTRODUCTION.

The Begonia family is not only an exceedingly large and most interesting one, but it is also very distinct, standing, from a botanical point of view, almost alone, and consisting of but two genera—the true Begonias and the genus *Hillebrandia*. Over three hundred and fifty distinct species of Begonia are known to the botanist, but of these only a few, comparatively speaking, are of any value from a horticultural point of view

By far the greater part of the Begonias in cultivation may be classed into three well-defined groups, viz : (1) The winter-flowering, fibrous-rooted section, comprising such varieties as *B. semperflorens, B. nitida,* and *B. Carrieri ;* (2) the ornamental leaved, or "Rex" class, which are grown almost entirely for the sake of their large and beautifully marked foliage; and (3) the tuberous-rooted, summer-flowering section, the individuals comprised in which have attained such popularity as decorative plants during the last few years, and of which these articles will principally treat. Of the three groups mentioned, the first two, though of undoubted value in their way, are vastly inferior in general utility, as well as in effectiveness, to the third, which, though the most recently introduced, has already far out-distanced the others in popularity. As a matter of fact, no other flowering plant has ever made such rapid and wonderful strides in general favour as this, the tuberous-rooted Begonia. There are also a considerable number of other species and varieties in cultivation which cannot be properly classed in either of the three sections mentioned. Some of these have tuberous roots, while those

A

of others are fibrous, some are deciduous, and others ever-green, or nearly so; but these will be referred to later on. At present our business is with the large, summer-flowering tuberous section.

As decorative plants, whether in the open air or under glass, the modern hybrid forms of the tuberous Begonia are certainly unequalled, and, indeed, almost without a rival. No other flowering plant in cultivation has ever been improved in such a rapid and really marvellous manner, as regards the size, colouring, and general beauty of the flowers, or has ever advanced so greatly in popular favour, and in so short a time, as this. Only a few years ago these Begonias were scarcely known, except here and there as botanical curiosities, while now they are grown and sold to the number of several millions annually. Even the zonal pelargonium cannot boast such a wide range of colouring—which in the Begonia includes pure yellow, bronze, and many exquisite shades of salmon, apricot, fawn, etc., as well as the whole of the hues, such as pure and blush white, pink, rose, orange, scarlet, crimson, etc., represented by the zonal—nor yet such a profuse and per-sistent habit of flowering. Other advantages possessed by the tuberous Begonia are that the roots, which go to rest in the autumn and remain dormant throughout the winter, require at that season neither light nor heat (except just enough to exclude frost) and very little care, being as easily preserved as so many potatoes in any frost-proof cupboard or cellar; and secondly, that when grown in the open air, the flowers are absolutely uninjured by wet or stormy weather. They are, indeed, the very best "wet-weather" flowers in cultivation, remaining bright and gay as ever when the geraniums have scarcely a petal left, and petunias and others are like so many washed-out rags. The only thing the Begonias cannot endure is actual frost, of which a very few degrees destroys the top growth in much the same manner as it affects dahlias, and effectually checks all progress for the remainder of the season. If it reaches the tubers at any time they are at once and entirely destroyed. After a certain stage of growth has been reached, these Begonias also flower unfailingly at every joint until the end of the season, whatever the weather or treatment may be.

In all probability it is chiefly as a bedding plant that the tuberous Begonia is destined to shine in the future. In the open air the plants succeed remarkably well during the summer months in almost any kind of soil, and few who have not seen them even fairly well done in this way would credit the gorgeous display of colouring they produce, even only under ordinarily advantageous circumstances. These Begonias are usually supposed to thrive best in a light or sandy soil, and to a certain extent this is the case, but the material with which I have to deal in a garden under my charge is a very heavy or clayey loam, and therefore much less suitable in several ways for anything of this kind than lighter formations; but I may mention that about the middle of last July I planted out several hundreds of seedlings that had been sown in the preceding March and were not pricked out until the beginning of May. No more preparation was afforded the beds beyond just digging them over and working in a moderate dressing of half-decayed manure. Drills about 3in deep were drawn with a trowel, and filled with a mixture of fine sandy soil, leaf-mould, and burnt earth, just to give the seedlings a start. The plants which were of course quite small, but sturdy and well hardened, were planted out direct from the boxes at about 6in. distance apart in the rows, these being some 9in. or 10in. apart. In spite of the exceedingly wet, cold, and stormy weather experienced during the autumn, the little plants grew rapidly, most of them commencing to flower in August, and during the whole of September and part of October the beds were a perfect blaze of intense colouring that quite surprised all who saw them. Had the plants been more forward by five or six weeks, and got out proportionately earlier into a rather lighter soil, and with more favourable weather, they would have done much better still, naturally; but I only mention this to show how freely these charming plants thrive and blossom in the open air, even under decidedly unfavourable conditions.

When thus cultivated out-of-doors they develop a sturdiness of growth, with a breadth and thickness of leaf and substance of petal, that they seldom attain under glass except under the most skilful cultivation, and at the same time they require a minimum of care, all that is necessary beyond a little weeding being to keep the soil constantly

moist until the plants become thoroughly established Even
the double-flowering varieties succeed in a remarkable
manner when thus planted out in suitable soil and with a
pure atmosphere around them. Mr. Gumbleton, of Belgrove,
Ireland, a well-known Begonia fancier, pointed this out
some year or two ago in the pages of the *Garden*, stating
that in this way even the finest named doubles succeeded
with him far better than in pots under glass. The moist
and genial atmosphere of the Emerald Isle is of course
peculiarly suited to the growth of these plants, but I
have proved the same thing repeatedly myself, both before
and since. For choice named double varieties I should,
however, prefer slightly-raised beds of specially prepared
soil in a lightly-shaded spot, as where the shadow of
distant trees fell during the middle of the day in summer.

As pot plants for the decoration of the conservatory or
greenhouse, the value of the tuberous Begonia has for some
time been tolerably well recognised. When well grown
they afford a simply gorgeous display of colour for months
together, and from the beginning or middle of June require
little or no artificial heat until the end of September, though
the means of applying a little warmth in this way certainly
prolongs the season considerably, and at both ends. This
renders them admirable subjects for the cold or unheated greenhouse, as the tubers may be wintered in a warm cupboard in
the house, and started in a frame or sunny window, when
the plants will succeed perfectly throughout the summer,
and blossom abundantly for three or four consecutive months.

The drooping-flowered varieties also make admirable
basket-plants, and they are moreover very suitable for
outside window-boxes, for vases in the open air, balconies,
and numerous other purposes. They may even be cultivated
in a light window, as room plants, with considerable success,
though it is only fair to say that they do not thrive in this
or indeed any other position in the smoky atmosphere of
large cities, as in the purer air and under the clearer skies
of a country spot.

The whole of the tuberous-rooted Begonias now in cultivation are really hybrids obtained by intercrossing six
original species—*B. boliviensis*, *B Veitchii*, *B. rosæflora*,
B. Davisii, *B. Clarkei*, and *B Pearcei*. All these are
natives of South America, Peru, and Bolivia, and were first

introduced during the years 1864-1876. Our present race of garden hybrids owe the greater part of their parentage to *B. boliviensis* and *B. Veitchii*; *B. rosæflora* and *B. Clarkei* having been but sparingly employed by the hybridist. The dwarf, erect-flowering varieties, both single and double, now so much esteemed, derive many of their characteristics from *B. Davisii*, a low-growing, erect-flowered species with bright scarlet blossoms. *B. Pearcei*, with beautifully marbled dark green foliage and small yellow flowers, is the source from which nearly all those with yellow or orange-coloured blossoms have been derived. Oddly enough, *B. Fræbeli*, a species with rather small hirsute cordate foliage and bright scarlet blossoms on erect foot-stalks, has persistently refused to ally itself with any of the others, though it comes fairly true from seed. Could this have been crossed with any other species, a distinct race would doubtless have resulted

The tuberous Begonia is a succulent, half-hardy, herbaceous plant, the roots or tubers being perennial, and the stems strictly annual. The leaves are oblique (hence the common name of Elephant's Ears), and the flowers are produced, usually in groups of three, six, or nine, on rather long peduncles springing from the axils of the leaves. The plants are also monœcious; that is to say, the male and female, or seed-bearing flowers, are distinct, and both are found on the same plant. The male flowers have usually four petals, of which the upper and lower ones are larger than the others, with a central mass of pollen-bearing anthers; while the female blossoms have five equal petals, with a three-celled (occasionally two, four, or more) and winged ovary, or seed-pod, immediately below them (the petals), and six curious corkscrew-shaped processes (arranged in three pairs) which really form the stigma in the centre. In each group of three flowers, each of which have their separate pedicels, the middle is usually a male or barren flower, and those on each side female; but often one of these outer blossoms will be a male also, and occasionally both of them. In the double-flowering varieties the male flowers alone are compound, the female blossoms being invariably single, and in both the single and double kinds the female flowers are, with very few exceptions, smaller and more insignificant than the others.

CHAPTER II.

GENERAL CULTURE.

THE tuberous Begonia is propagated chiefly in two ways, viz., from seeds, and by means of cuttings. Seedlings make the best and most vigorous plants, but when increased by means of cuttings, the plants come perfectly true to the parent ; while seedlings always vary more or less, hence this method (that of cuttings) is always employed when increasing named varieties. By either method tubers are produced after the plants have been in growth a short time, and these retain their vitality, if not exposed to actual frost, for several years, increasing in size annually, and producing taller and thicker stems and more flowers each year also, though the blossoms decrease in size to some extent after the second season.

The seed being very small, to raise plants in this way with any degree of certainty is a somewhat delicate matter, requiring some amount of experience and skill, with suitable appliances, while cuttings also often fail to strike if the conditions are not exactly right. The best way for the inexperienced amateur is therefore to purchase the corms or tubers, which can be had either in a dormant state or just starting into growth, from December to April or May. One-year-old roots should always be preferred, as they have their life before them, while older tubers will be deteriorating year by year. When at rest, or only just starting, the tubers are easily packed in a very small compass, and will travel any distance with perfect safety, except of course during severe frost. It is worthy of note that while seedling tubers are nearly or quite round, convex on the bottom, and more or less concave or hollow on the top, those obtained from cuttings are very irregular in form. Seedling tubers must always be planted with the hollow side, from which the stems spring, uppermost; but it is often impossible to tell the top from the bottom of tubers raised from cuttings until they start into growth.

Although these plants will thrive more or less well in almost any kind of soil, light or heavy—at least when planted out-of-doors—and, as has already been seen, they succeed remarkably well even in quite a clayey staple, yet they attain their greatest luxuriance in a free, mellow, and moderately-rich material, preferably of a loamy character Something of this kind is absolutely necessary for plants in pots, mixing it of course with a little good leaf-mould or well-decayed manure as the case may be, and, if necessary, some sand also. I have even potted the plants in pure loam of good quality only, and then had them succeed well with the aid of some liquid manure when pot-bound Peat is, as a rule, undesirable for this class of Begonia, though it suits the fibrous-rooted varieties excellently; but the tuberous-rooted kinds make a decidedly longer and weaker growth in this material than in loam, or a compost consisting principally of the latter. At the same time the more delicate rooted double varieties, especially when grown from cuttings, evidently enjoy a small proportion of peat—a third or fourth of the whole—and make both roots and growth more freely in such a compost than in a too substantial one. At one time nearly pure leaf-mould was thought to be the right thing for them, and I remember purchasing a batch of large flowering plants that were potted in nothing but this material and sand, but though they did well for a time they soon went off. While the plants are in a young state there is nothing better than leaf-mould, but after a certain stage has been reached it is not sufficiently substantial for them. Spent hops, again, is an excellent thing for these plants, whether growing out-of-doors or in pots; it should be used in a half-decayed condition, and with an equal quantity of loam and some sand will grow them to perfection.

Plenty of fresh air, and of light also, are of the greatest importance in the culture of these Begonias. During the early stages, both in raising seedlings and when starting the tubers, a moderately warm and moist atmosphere, with limited ventilation, considerably accelerates their progress, and to a certain extent increases the vigour of the growth; but after the first flower-buds appear at the latest, free and even abundant ventilation should be the rule, and to treat them as stove-plants is a great mistake and certain to end in failure. The more light the plants receive also the better they thrive, and to this end they should always be kept moderately near the glass; indeed, in the spring and autumn there is no better place for them than a high shelf within a foot or two of the roof; but though in the open air they can endure the rays of the hottest sun uninjured, yet under glass, if not screened in some way from strong sunshine in summer, they will scorch, and the petals wilt or wither, so that a light and preferably movable shading should always be provided.

Again, these Begonias enjoy a fair share of moisture at nearly all periods of growth. While dormant, the tubers should be kept moderately but not excessively dry, and when starting them, until some roots have been formed, and a couple of inches or so of growth has been made, it is best to keep them rather on the dry side, or decay may set in; but once fairly in growth, the soil must never be allowed to become thoroughly dry, or the vigour of the plant will be lost for the season. An excess of moisture must be guarded against in the case of pot plants—a sodden or waterlogged soil being fatal; but in the open ground the plants appear to be capable of enduring almost any amount of moisture.

If sown early in the year, seedling plants flower freely the same season. By sowing in heat in January, and pushing the plants on as fast as possible, I have even had them in flower, in 4½in. pots, in June; but there is no difficulty in getting seedlings raised in February, or even the early part of March, in full flower during August and September, either in pots or the open ground. Seedlings, at least when well grown, make very neat plants of a dwarf habit of growth, and begin flowering much nearer the ground than old tubers; hence, for small beds or edgings they are excellent, and particularly useful for late or autumn flowering; but for all ordinary purposes one-year-old tubers are the best. Oddly enough seedlings of the double varieties begin flowering considerably sooner than the singles. If the seed is carefully saved from distinct types of any particular colour, the parent plants being isolated from those of any

other colour, the progeny will come fairly true   Thus, if
one takes, say, two plants with crimson or pink flowers of
as nearly as possible the same shade, habit, etc., placing
them in a house or pit by themselves, and cross-fertilises
the blossoms in a proper manner, eighty or ninety per cent.
of the plants raised from the seed so obtained will produce
flowers of the same colour; but when the different colours are
mixed together in the same house the seedlings will vary
greatly.

Lastly, an error that most people fall into is that of pre-
ferring large bulbs to small ones.   In any batch of seedlings
some of the plants will germinate more quickly, grow faster
and stronger (at first), and form much larger bulbs in a
given time than others; but with few exceptions such are
always of inferior quality, and by far the largest proportion
of first-class flowers, and always the best, will be found
among the later and weaker seedlings, which, of course, form
comparatively small bulbs the first season.   Many of these
may not blossom the first year at all, unless sown very early
and grown well, and hence small tubers should always be
preferred to larger ones of the same age.   Very large tubers
I regard as of little use except to afford large specimen
plants for exhibition or the like, and, as previously stated,
after the second season the flowers decrease in size annually.
To produce flowers of the largest size and finest quality,
one-year-old tubers that were planted out in the open ground
the previous summer, and grown in 7in. or 8in. pots the
following year, will afford the best results.

CHAPTER III.

CULTURE IN POTS.

For early flowering—in May or the early part of June—
the tubers should be started in a moderate heat early in
February. March is a good month in which to make a
start, though in this case the flowers are of course somewhat later; some even place the tubers in heat towards the
end of January, but when forced so early the growth is
comparatively weak and the flowers smaller than if the
plants are brought along more naturally. Choice named
varieties or selected seedlings should be placed singly in
pots of about twice the diameter (internally) of the tubers;
give rather free drainage, and use a light, porous, and
sandy compost, such as a mixture of equal parts of fine
loam, leaf-mould, cocoa-nut fibre, and sharp or coarse sand.
The fibre is very useful during the early stages of growth,
encouraging as it does the formation of roots, and rendering the soil thoroughly porous; but it should be borne in
mind that it contains little or no actual nutriment. Pot
loosely, *i e*, do not press the soil down much, particularly
in dealing with the single varieties, which produce very
coarse roots at first, a tap or two of the pot on the bench
being quite sufficient to settle the soil. Make a shallow
hole for the tuber with the finger, putting in a pinch of
sand for it to rest on, and barely cover the crown, a pinch
of pure sand or cocoa-nut fibre being quite sufficient. If
possible the pots should be plunged in a moderate hot-
bed, 70deg. to 75deg. being a good mean for the bottom
heat, with 5deg. or even 10deg. less overhead. Keep the
soil almost dry until some roots have been formed and the
growth has fairly commenced, tor if kept too moist the

tubers will decay, but they may be sprinkled overhead on fine days with advantage. As soon as the young shoots appear keep the plants in full light, as near the glass as may be convenient or safe, but with light shade from strong sunshine, and the roots in an even and moderate state of moisture. The tubers will start, though rather more slowly, on a shelf or stage in any warm house or pit; in such places, however, the soil is apt to get very dry unless carefully attended, but remember that too much water is almost as bad as not enough.

Directly the roots begin to work round the sides of the first pots the plants must be shifted into others about 1½in. larger; that is to say, if started in 3in. pots they should now have the 4½in. size, or what are known as "small forty-eights"; if they now occupy 3½in. pots, give them the 5in. or "large forty-eights," and so on. For this potting a rather more substantial compost should be employed, two parts of good fibrous loam to one part of leaf-mould, a dash of cocoa-nut fibre and coarse sand being very suitable; a little of some good artificial manure, such as Thomson's, may also be now added with advantage. Some use decayed stable manure, but if employed at all for pot plants it must be well rotted and rendered perfectly sweet and flaky by long exposure to a dry atmosphere. For my own part, I seldom employ it except a very little for large specimen plants, preferring to depend for extra nourishment upon liquid manure and stimulants. Except for the first potting, do not sift the soil; simply break up the lumps of loam with the hand, and pick out any bits of stick or stones from the leaf-mould. Use the rougher parts of the compost below, over the drainage, and the finer towards the surface. If the loam is very fine and inclined to go "pasty," use a fair proportion of fresh cocoa-nut fibre, but remember that this material must always be sifted before use, as, though excellent in itself, Begonias and all plants appear to entertain a strong antipathy to the "hairs" or fibre proper; it is, in fact, the "refuse" only that is of any value in the garden. Do not press the soil too hard, especially if the plants are to be shifted on again, though if they are intended to flower in these pots it may be made moderately firm, and the doubles ought always to have a rather more compact root-run, as well as somewhat

finer soil, than the single kinds.   Choice doubles of the
new erect-flowering varieties in particular may with great
benefit have a third or fourth part of good sandy peat
added to the compost.

After potting, keep the plants rather warm and close for
about a week, and dew them lightly overhead on fine
mornings, but only give sufficient water to keep the soil
barely moist until it is occupied by the new roots.   If
convenient, the plants may be returned to the hot-bed for
a short time ; but in case this cannot be done, they ought to
have been withdrawn and gradually used to standing " free "
on a shelf or stage for a week or so before being repotted.

During the early part of the season these Begonias,
which at all times enjoy a moderate warmth, though they
dislike strong heat, need a temperature slightly above that
of an ordinary greenhouse in order to make satisfactory
progress.   After about the beginning of May they succeed
well enough under ordinary greenhouse treatment, but up
to about this time they thrive best in what is known as an
intermediate temperature, along with gloxinias, etc , at
least until the flower-buds begin to appear, when more air
must be given

The size of the pots in which the plants are to be flowered
depends in part upon the size and natural vigour of the
tubers, in part upon the space at command, and to some
extent upon the treatment.   Good-sized one-year-old
seedling tubers that were grown in the open ground the
first season (and these almost invariably give the best
results) may be potted on until 8in. or even 9in. pots are
required, supposing that large specimens are desired and
can be found room for, while older plants with several
stems will need larger sizes still, but as a rule the amateur
grower will find 6in and 7in. pots the most convenient
sizes in which to flower the majority of the plants, particularly where the greenhouse is small.   When a quantity of
blossom, without so much regard to the size of either the
flowers or the plants, is the object, it is better to keep the
plants in comparatively small sizes, the vigour being maintained by the frequent use of weak liquid manure. In order
to obtain large specimens, it is absolutely necessary that the
plants be potted on into larger sizes directly the roots
begin to work round the sides of the first, and before they

become anything like full or pot-bound, for this throws them into flower directly, and then it is lifficult, if not impossible to get them to make any amount of growth afterwards.

The larger the pots the rougher should the soil be, a number of good-sized lumps of turfy-loam placed over the drainage being highly beneficial, especially when filling the larger sizes. The potting should also be done rather more firmly at each shift, using the rougher parts of the compost below and the finer towards the surface. A moderate proportion of half-decayed, spent hops may now be used with advantage, both mixed with the soil and over the drainage, and a 6in. potful of Thomson's or other good artificial fertiliser should be added to and well mixed with each barrowful of compost. A little thoroughly-decayed manure may also be employed when potting large plants, but it must be very sweet and flaky, and on the whole I prefer the hops or good leaf-mould. Take care that the ball of soil is in a moderately moist condition when a plant is shifted into a larger pot, and to this end they should have been watered a few hours previously. A little weak stimulant is often very useful at this stage—just before potting the plants on.

Ventilation is a most important point. In fine warm weather these Begonias can scarcely get enough air, and from the beginning or middle of June (according to the season) until the middle or end of September the roof-ventilators, at least of a small house, ought scarcely ever to be entirely closed by day or night, unless the weather is stormy or unseasonably cold. The size of the structure should, however, be taken into consideration in ventilating, as plants standing in a roomy or lofty house will naturally bear to be kept somewhat closer at times than others occupying only a small or low place. Never take a lot of air off suddenly towards the close of a fine day, according to a very common practice; nothing is more likely to cause the buds or blossoms to drop prematurely than this, especially if the house is damped down at the same time Air should also be given freely at the sides or front of the house in calm and warm periods, but avoid through draughts, which are usually injurious In fine, the more hardily these Begonias are grown and treated throughout the better, as.

though they may not advance quite so rapidly, the growth is shorter and more sturdy and bushy, and the flowers possess more substance and last longer, even if they do not become actually larger also, than in a close and warm atmosphere.

Watering, also, must be very carefully and regularly attended to. Except in very hot weather, when it may be done at almost any time, the forenoon is the best period of the day to give water, as then the stems and foliage become dry by nightfall In a low temperature, and especially towards the autumn when the nights grow long and cool, a single drop of water lying on the stem or leaf throughout the night will frequently eat a hole into or right through the tissue, and thus set up decay, which may end in the total loss of the branch, or even of the entire plant Consequently, unless evaporation, caused by either artificial heat or natural means, is sufficiently active to prevent such an occurrence, care must be taken that every part of the plant, above the soil at least, is perfectly dry by sunset. Overhead watering, or the use of the syringe, is, however, seldom necessary, at least after the plants have begun flowering, though a light sprinkle occasionally will refresh them considerably in very hot or dry weather, and in all ordinarily fine periods the floor, paths, stages, etc., should be damped down once or twice daily. During the early stages, however, the overhead shower with syringe or fine-rosed can will be found to assist and accelerate the growth. In giving water at the root, the rule is the same as for nearly all other plants under pot culture, viz., to give none until the soil shows slight signs of dryness, and then to afford a thorough supply, enough to wet every particle of soil and root down to the bottom of the pot. Clean rain-water should always be used when obtainable, and let it be of as nearly as possible the same temperature as the house itself when applied ; if hard water must be employed, it should stand in an open tank exposed to the sun for a day or two at least before being used, and a little soda (the nitrate is best, but ordinary washing soda will do) added will also help to soften it

Plants in full blossom, with the pots crammed with roots, require a lot of water, particularly in hot weather ; they ought then never to be allowed to get really dry, and, with free drainage, there will be but little danger of giving too much. Such as have been recently potted, or are but imperfectly rooted, must, however, be very sparingly watered for a time, and towards the end of the season, when the flowers are getting over and the tubers going to rest, the supply of water must also be gradually reduced until the soil becomes quite dry

Plants standing on shelves or open stages are apt to become very dry in warm weather, especially if there are hot-water pipes or a flue beneath or near them, so that in the height of summer, or if much artificial heat is used, it is best to place them on a bed of ashes, cocoa-nut fibre, or the like, this being kept constantly moist; but early as well as late in the season, or when grown in a cool or unheated house, they will thrive better on an open staging, formed of narrow boards or laths, with a space of 1in. or so between each.

It is a somewhat curious but undoubted fact that these Begonias thrive better, as a rule, in a roomy or lofty house than in a small or low one The fact is they cannot endure a confined atmosphere, and, except to a slight extent during the early stages, the only chance of succeeding really well with them in structures of small cubic capacity is to ventilate as freely as possible, and in fact to keep a gentle current of air always passing through the plants

Shading from all hot or strong sunshine is necessary to the production of healthy and handsome plants and fine, well-developed flowers. In the open air the plants will stand any amount of sun when a little used to it, though a hot, bright day or two succeeding a dull period sometimes causes them to flag or wilt to some extent; but unless protected from the fierce rays of the sun, plants under glass will quickly become scorched and the edges of the petals wither. A proper blind fixed on a roller is much the best thing, as it can be taken off when not actually required, and the plants thus receive the full benefit of the light in the early mornings and evenings, as well as in wet or dull weather; but, failing this, some white or lime wash brushed over the glass will answer the purpose tolerably well. The preparation known as "Summer Cloud" is excellent, and flour and water (not paste) with a very little whiting added can also be recommended, as when wet it becomes semi-transparent, and though easily removed when required it is not readily washed off by rain. A span-roofed structure running east and west is a good place for Begonias; for a movable blind on the south side will afford nearly all the shade required, and a light sprinkling of whitewash on the north face in the height of summer will break the sun's rays sufficiently in the early mornings and evenings. The blind ought never to be brought into use until really required, and directly the sun falls so low in the sky as to be no longer dangerous it should be drawn up again, overmuch or heavy shading tending to weaken the plants, and being therefore decidedly injurious.

Ripening and Storing the Tubers.—Towards the
end of the season, when the plants are getting past their best, the chief object should be to get the tubers thoroughly matured or ripened. To this end the supply of water must be gradually reduced, and the plants be exposed as fully as possible to the influences of fresh air and sunshine—by degrees, of course. The best plan, indeed, if the season is not too far advanced, is to remove the plants altogether into the open air, standing them on a bed of ashes on a sunny yet sheltered spot; care must, however, be taken that they do not get caught by early autumn frosts, certainly not to such an extent as to penetrate the pots, or the tubers will be irretrievably ruined. A sojourn of three or four weeks in the open air not only increases the size of the tubers considerably, but renders them much more firm and substantial also, so that they winter more safely, and start away the following spring with much greater vigour.

Take the plants inside again before they have been affected by more frost than just sufficient to touch the tops; but still keep them quite cool and with abundance of air, and as the short days of winter draw on, the leaves and stems will fall away by degrees until nothing but the tubers are left in the soil. This ought now to be quite dry, and as soon as convenient the tubers should be shaken out of the soil and be stored away in any frost-proof and moderately-dry place, named or marked varieties singly in small pots, with a little cocoa-nut fibre around them, the label being stuck in against the side of each, and mixed kinds together in a box or large pot, with a little of the material just mentioned to prevent them bruising each other as well as to check too rapid evaporation. As when first taken from the soil the skin of the tubers is very tender, care should be taken not to remove any when rubbing away the earth; but after a time it becomes more firm or "set," and the roots may then be handled with impunity. Some growers store the roots away in the soil and pots as they grow, laying them on their sides under a greenhouse stage or elsewhere; but my objection to this plan is that it is difficult to tell in what condition the tubers are, while when stored in fibre they can be examined at any time damping them (or the fibre) if too dry, and placing them in a drier and warmer place should they have become too moist from any cause.

A fairly warm cellar is a good place in which to store the tubers, or failing this they may be kept under the stage in a greenhouse (but not too near hot pipes or a flue), or even in a cupboard in a kitchen or other room to which actual frost does not gain entrance. Extremes of both heat and cold, moisture and dryness, should be carefully avoided as being highly injurious and often fatal.

If, instead of being dried and ripened off, the plants are kept in a genial temperature during the autumn, they will, especially if they were started and potted late, continue to grow and flower more or less freely until the middle or end of November, and a batch of such late-flowering plants are often very useful, but the tubers do not, as a rule, ripen so well, nor start so early in the spring as those that have gone to rest earlier. Seedling plants raised in February or the beginning of March are admirably adapted for late flowering, and with a fair amount of warmth and a little feeding, etc, afford a capital display during the months of October and November, and sometimes later still, the plants occupying 5in. or at the outside 6in pots. At this season they require a very light position near the glass, and no shade.

Treatment of Small Tubers.—Plants from seed sown after March at the latest seldom flower to any extent the same season, but form small tubers, which, if started early the following spring and grown on for a time under glass,

B

make excellent plants for bedding-out, as well as flowering
capitally in 5in. or 6in. pots during the summer. As the
seed nearly always germinates more or less irregularly, such
seedlings as are picked off last, or late in the season, also
frequently fail to flower the first year, but generally do
remarkably well the second. I have several thousands of
such "unblossomed seedlings" annually, and it is a curious
but indisputable fact that it is among these later and
smaller seedlings that the finest flowers almost always
appear. Such small or late tubers continue to grow longer
than the more forward plants, and should be kept moving
on gently in a moderate warmth until the foliage dies away,
which often does not take place until towards Christmas.
They should be wintered in the pots or boxes in which they
grew, and in a temperature of not less than 45deg. to
50deg., while the soil ought not to be allowed to become
very dry at any time. Start them early in the spring by
placing them, without disturbance, in a warm house or pit,
and if possible on a moderately hot bed, in February or the
early part of March. Water them very sparingly until an
inch or so of growth has been made, when the soil must be
kept constantly moist, and then transfer them singly to
small (2½in. or 3in.) pots, grown on in a genial temperature,
and either shift into larger pots when ready or harden off
and plant out of doors in June. If obtained from a distance,
or from any cause they have been shaken out of the soil,
the best way to treat such small tubers is to lay them out
about 1½in. apart on the surface of a box or pan of light,
porous, sandy soil (such as a mixture of equal parts of loam,
leaf-soil, cocoa-nut fibre, and coarse sand), half-full of rough
stuff for drainage, and barely covering the crowns with
sandy soil on cocoa-nut fibre Keep moderately close and
warm, with shade from strong sun, but the soil not too
moist until well in growth, then pot up singly as above.

Liquid Manures and Stimulants.—Although
these Begonias cannot be correctly termed gross feeders,
yet it is impossible to grow them to perfection in
pots without the aid of liquid and other stimulating
manures. Care must, however, be taken not to employ
anything of this kind to excess, or more harm than good
will result, so that some amount of caution is necessary. In

"feeding" these plants the cultivator should be guided by the same rules as apply in the case of any others, that is to say : (1) Such stimulants must only be given when the plants are in a more or less pot-bound condition (*i.e.*, the pots fairly full of roots); (2) apply the stimulant frequently in mild doses rather than run any risk of injury by giving it too strong at any time; (3) vary the nature of the fertiliser as much as possible; and, lastly, always afford at least one watering with the pure liquid between two applications of the stimulant

Soot water is an excellent thing for these and nearly all other pot plants, but it must be used both *weak* and *clean*. A teaspoonful or two to each gallon of water is sufficient, if thoroughly dissolved, but do not give even this too frequently, once a week is quite often enough, and unless the plants are in full growth and bloom, too often, indeed. When kept in a moist condition, soot dissolves readily in water, but the best way is to sink a small bagful (with a stone in it) in the water tank, and poke it about with a stick occasionally ; this gives just a blackish tinge to the water, and such a weak infusion may be used regularly, or nearly so, while the plants are in blossom.

The liquid from a stable or farmyard, or that made by steeping the nearly fresh but partially dried droppings of horses, or better still, that of sheep, is excellent, but it must be diluted so as to appear of the colour of very weak tea only, and if applied too frequently even at this strength it will promote an undue amount of growth at the expense of blossom.

A weak solution of sulphate of ammonia or nitrate of soda, given occasionally, imparts a considerable impetus to the growth of the plants, while the former also increases the size and beauty of the flowers ; but both being of very rapid and powerful action, they should be employed with great care and caution, once in every two or three weeks, and then only while the plants are in full growth and blossom, being quite often enough to give it. Half-an-ounce of either salt to each gallon of water is strong enough, and in fact it is better to begin with ½oz. only, and gradually increase the strength. Thomson's vine and plant manure, applied as a top-dressing at the rate of a teaspoonful to a 6in. pot, sprinkling it on the surface of the soil, and then lightly pricking and watering it in, is a capital fertiliser for these Begonias, and may be given about twice during the season with the best results; or a small proportion—say, a 5in. potful to a barrowload of compost—may be mixed with the soil when potting the plants into any of the larger sizes. The patent silicate manure also exercises a marked effect upon both the growth and the inflorescence if employed in the same manner as the last, but in rather more liberal quantity.

CHAPTER IV.

PROPAGATION.

THE tuberous Begonia is chiefly propagated in two ways :
(1) By means of seed, and (2) by striking cuttings of the
shoots. Leaf cuttings are also occasionally employed, but
they are difficult to strike, and even when tubers have been
obtained they not infrequently refuse to grow altogether.
Named kinds of these Begonias are invariably increased by
means of cuttings, for in no other way can they be kept true
to character and name. Seedlings, however carefully the
seed may have been saved, always vary more or less among
themselves, and also differ to a considerable extent from the
parent plants, but they are generally much more robust and
vigorous in growth than plants raised from cuttings, and as
a rule should receive the preference, especially for bedding
and all ordinary decorative purposes. Again, many of the
finest varieties produce cuttings but sparingly, so that it is
some years before sufficient stock can be obtained to enable
them to be sold at a moderate price, and by that time the
" strain" will probably have been so much improved by
means of careful selection, that many of the seedlings will
be quite equal, in point of quality, to the cutting plants,
and some very likely even superior, while they are certain
to possess far more vigour.

Sowing the Seed.—The seed of the Begonia being exceedingly small—at first sight it appears more like so much
brown dust or snuff than anything else—it must be sown on
a very finely-sifted surface, and the seedlings be treated
with the greatest care during the early stages, though after
a certain stage is reached the young plants are little if at

all more troublesome than any others.   The chief points to
be observed in the successful raising of these Begonias from
seed are : (1) A genial but even temperature, a range of
65deg. to 70deg being most suitable and, on the whole,
better than a stronger heat, even 5deg. less will do , (2) a
moderate, even, and regular condition of moisture in the
soil, which, though it ought seldom to become really wet,
must not be allowed to get thoroughly dry at any time
during the period of germination, or this will be effectually
checked, and the sowing fail altogether ; (3) a light and rich
yet perfectly sweet soil, sifted very fine upon the surface,
and extra well drained ; (4) shade from all direct sunshine
until the plants gain a certain degree of size and strength ;
and (5) prick off the seedlings singly as soon as ever they
can be handled, and by preference while the first "rough"
or proper leaf (beyond the cotyledons) is in process of
formation.

After a long experience I find no other description of soil
equal, for raising these Begonias or any other plants with
minute seeds, nearly pure leaf-mould.   This does not readily
become green on the surface as peat will do, nor does it cake
as both loam and sand are almost sure to do, while it
contains abundance of nutriment and produces stout and
healthy seedlings with plenty of active roots. It should,
however, be well baked, or even partially burnt or charred
before use, in order to destroy any insects or their eggs,
fungoid germs, or the like.

Fill a pot (the 6in. size is a very convenient one) or pan
half-full of crocks or bricks broken small—fresh coal (not
coke) cinders, or some moderately rough "ballast" (burnt
clay) will do as well—and on this a thick layer of moss or
rough siftings of the soil. Little more than 1in in depth
of a mixture of leaf-mould with a fourth part each of fine
loam, cocoa-nut fibre, and coarse sand, the whole well
mixed and run through a ½in. sieve, must come next, then
press it gently to an even level, water well with a fine rose,
and ten minutes afterwards add a bare ¼in. of pure leaf-
mould that has been well baked and passed through a very
fine wire or hair sieve. If after a short time it is seen that
this fine surface material has not become moistened by
absorption from that below, it must be lightly sprinkled
with a fine rose   Now sow the seed, scattering it evenly

and not too thickly over the surface, for if fresh and good nearly every grain will germinate, and when the seedlings stand very thickly they are more liable to damp off, as well as to become weak and drawn if not pricked off almost as soon as up. Being so very fine the seed should be barely covered with the merest dusting of fine soil (not sand, which soon becomes caked and green); some growers do not cover it at all. Lay a sheet of white-washed glass, or a plain square with a piece of paper on it, over the pot or pan, and plunge, if possible, in a hot-bed at 70deg. to 75deg., or failing this the seed will germinate, though not quite so quickly or well, in any moderately warm house, pit, or frame. Take care to shade from sun, and examine the pots or pans daily as to moisture. When water is needed, give it very gently through a fine rose, or stand the pot or pan in water nearly up to the level of the soil; the former, if properly performed, is the better plan. Always use clean rain or soft water, with just the chill off, or at the same temperature as the plants are growing in Remove the glass for an hour or so morning and evening, for if kept too close a kind of white mildew forms on the surface of the soil, and destroys the tiny seedlings. As soon as the seed has fairly germinated, and the young plants are in growth, the glass must be gradually removed altogether.

The sooner the seedlings can be pricked off singly after the first rough or proper leaf appears the better. This must be done into other pans or boxes, prepared much as before, placing them about 1in apart, or even less This is tedious work, but it must be done, and done with care, each seedling being lifted singly, and with every bit of root uninjured, and as carefully transferred to the "store" pan. A very small, flat-pointed piece of wood (such as a label) should be used to lift the tiny plants with, another with a round blunt end (a large match will do for this) to make the holes, and a third piece cut to a very fine flat point, with a V-shaped notch in the end will be found useful to lift the seedlings with, and much better than attempting to lay hold of them with the fingers. As each pan or box is finished, water it well and place in a nice growing temperature, taking care that the soil never becomes dry, and shading carefully from the sun. Some sheets of glass laid loosely over them for the first week or

so also helps the young plants to establish themselves, but
they should be supported an inch or two above the rims of
the pans or boxes by strips of wood, and not lie down too
closely. If the seedlings are left too long in the seed-pan
they are not only apt to damp off wholesale, but even if
this does not occur the disturbance of the roots after they
have run a little way administers a check that they do not
soon recover.

As the seedlings gain size and strength, and the weather
becomes warmer, let them have more air and a little sun,
but not too strong ; reduce the fire heat, and directly they
begin to touch each other transfer them to other boxes
filled with leaf-mould, loam, and sand in a rather rough
condition, and not quite so freely drained as before. This
time they may be placed 1½in. or 2in apart; again keep
them moderately close and shaded for a time, and supposing
them to have been pricked off the first time in February or
the early part of March, early in May they should be
removed to cold frames to be gradually hardened off, and
finally plant them out, about 6in. apart, in rich mellow soil,
and an open and sunny position. This may be done at any
time after all danger of even a slight frost is over, say the
third or fourth week in June; I have even planted them
out as late as the second or third week in July, and then
obtained nice medium-sized tubers and a good many flowers

Another plan is to pot the seedlings off singly from the
store-boxes, growing them on under glass, and finally
either planting them out as before or shifting them on
into larger pots to flower. If this is done, 2½in. pots, or
what florists term "small sixties," should be employed in
the first place, and then if afterwards moved into 4½in. pots,
say, in June, they will flower beautifully during the latter
part of the summer and the autumn If very forward they
may be shifted first into 4in. pots, and subsequently into
the 6in size (thirty-two's), but it is not well to run any
risk of over-potting the seedlings the first season   Unless
it is desired to grow and flower the plants in pots throughout, the potting system demands considerably more space,
as well as labour, than that of growing them in boxes, and
if well hardened and carefully planted out from the latter
they succeed nearly or quite as well as from pots. Take
care that while in small pots the plants do not get very

dry at any time, as they are apt to do unless very carefully and thoroughly watered, especially when standing in a warm house, or on an open or dry staging over hot-water pipes.

If the seed is sown during the latter half of January or early in February, and the plants are kept growing on steadily in a genial warmth and with plenty of moisture, they ought to be ready to prick out in boxes in March, and to be re-boxed or potted some time during April. They should then be hardened off in May, and if planted out in June many of them will, if all goes well, begin flowering early in July, and during the months of August and September will make a grand display of blossom. I have even sown the seed in March, pricking off the seedlings about the end of April and planting them out the middle of July—a month later all round—and they have still done well, and flowered beautifully in September and even October, the weather remaining mild and open. If sown later than March they cannot, however, be expected to flower the same season, but either in boxes or small pots will make nice little tubers that will flower profusely during the whole of the following summer; the objection to this plan is that they cannot be selected to colour, etc., and must be employed in mixture only.

Those who have little or no heat at command may sow in May or the beginning of June, when the seed will germinate even in an unheated greenhouse, if covered with a sheet of glass and shaded, pricking off the seedlings into boxes in July. Keep them growing as long as possible, and if practicable store and start the tiny tubers next spring in the same soil and boxes in which they grew, and all will flower abundantly the following summer. Even under this system it is advisable to remove the boxes to the open air for three or four weeks in August or September, when the plants are pretty well established, as in this way they will make much sounder, as well as larger, tubers than if kept under glass altogether; but take care to house them again before they get even a slight touch of frost.

Striking Cuttings.—When propagated by means of cuttings, plants of these Begonias come perfectly true to the parents, hence this is the only method available in dealing with named varieties, or where it is desired to increase and preserve any particular or valuable kind, single or double. It is also by no means a difficult matter to root cuttings of the right description, if gone about in a proper manner, and if taken early in the season such cutting-plants soon commence flowering, and make a nice display the same year. Individual plants, however, vary considerably in the behaviour of their progeny when grown from cuttings, some retaining their vigour for years, and being largely increased in this way with little or no apparent detriment, while others deteriorate so rapidly as to be nearly or quite useless by the time the third or fourth generation is reached. This is why I generally and so strongly recommend good seedling Begonias in preference to "named kinds"—plants grown repeatedly from cuttings, however excellent at first, are certain to lose their vigour and consequently their value, sooner or later, however skilfully cultivated On the other hand, by selecting a few of the best plants to seed from annually, any collection or type may be considerably improved in the course of a few years, while the plants from cuttings are going back. At the same time it is worth while to increase anything particularly good or distinct in this way, at least for a time, or until signs of deterioration are perceived; and it is a curious but undoubted fact that cuttings of the double varieties, as a rule, are not only more easily rooted than those of the single kinds, but that they last longer, and give much better results generally than the latter.

Any particularly good double flowering Begonias may be pretty safely depended upon to come and do well from cuttings for three or four years at least. As an example, that beautiful pure white double variety Octavie may be instanced; though raised now a good many years ago, and having been propagated from cuttings by the thousand, it is at the present time almost as vigorous and quite as floriferous as at first. An old pink double named Rosamonde also did remarkably well in this way, and was largely propagated, but it is now superseded by better forms.

There are three chief or principal ways by which cuttings of these Begonias may be rooted. Firstly, the young shoots that spring direct from the tubers when the latter start into growth in the spring, if taken off when 2in. or

3in. in length and inserted round the sides of well-drained pots of sandy soil, in much the same manner as cuttings of dahlias are treated, plunging them in a gentle hot-bed and keeping them moderately moist and shaded, very few will fail to root and make good plants, which will soon commence to flower and continue during the rest of the season. The only objection to the general adoption of this practice is that, unlike dahlias, the second crop of shoots is always very much weaker than the first, so that unless a tuber throws several growths, of which some can be taken as cuttings and the others left, to rob the roots in this way to any extent weakens and injures them considerably.

Secondly, any young growths springing from the base of the stem of a flowing plant may be taken off and struck in much the same manner as before, either in a very gentle hot-bed or in any house or pit that can be kept moderately warm and close at any time during the summer. If possible such cuttings should be taken off with a slight "heel," and be inserted either singly in "thumb" pots, or several together round the sides of a 3½in size; stand them in any rather close, shady, and generally "quiet" place under glass and water them very carefully until rooted and growing again. The more hard or firm all such cuttings are when taken, so long as they are in a growing state, the better, as they are less likely to "damp off," which is what must chiefly be guarded against, so that the plants from which they are taken should have had plenty of air and light for some time previously. When properly rooted pot them off singly, or if inserted in single pots give them a small "shift," and keep them rather close and shaded for a time, and even if they do not flower to any extent the same season they will form nice little tubers that will do good work the following year.

The third method is that of inserting the well-matured tops or side-shoots of any plants that have done flowering in a comparatively cool temperature towards the end of the season. About the end of July or the early part of August is the best time, as if inserted later the cuttings have not time to form roots and tubers before the winter sets in. The old plants should have been well ripened previously by standing them out in the open air for two or three weeks, if possible. It is not necessary for such cuttings to possess a "heel," though this is at all times an advantage, but if cut clean across just below a joint—the third or fourth, usually—that will do. The cuttings may be rooted in pots as before, but the best way is to make up a well-drained bed of nice free sandy soil, such as that recommended for starting the tubers in, in a frame or low pit; surface it with ½in. of pure sand, and in this dibble out the cuttings, placing them 2in. or 3in apart Keep the sashes almost closed at first, until the cuttings form a callus and begin to "stick up," when more air may be admitted, and in damp or dull weather a very little fire-heat will encourage growth and the production of roots, as well as tend to prevent damping. If only the lower end of the cutting hardens into a kind of tuber and emits a few roots, this will retain its vitality through the winter and start into growth again in the following spring.

Cuttings of Begonias ought always to be slightly dried before being inserted. In dull or cool weather they may be laid on a shelf for a few hours; but do not let them wilt badly under a strong sun. When struck in heat, a good plan is simply to let them lie on the cocoa-nut fibre surface of the hot-bed for a day or two, as here the cut will heal over, but the cuttings will not flag Tubers that have been grown from cuttings are always more or less irregularly formed—not round and even as seedling tubers almost invariably are.

Pots to receive the cuttings must be very carefully prepared, extra free drainage and a thoroughly porous and sandy soil being indispensable conditions. Half or one-third fill them (more in the case of large pots than small ones) with small pieces of broken brick or fresh coal-cinders, and over this place 1in. or so of moss, or of rough siftings, to prevent the soil being washed down among the drainage. Fill up to within ½in. of the rim with a free porous compost consisting of about equal parts of loam, leaf-mould, cocoa-nut fibre (sifted), and sand, and finish off with ¼in. to ½in. of pure silver sand. Water the cuttings in well after insertion, but let them just dry again before placing them in the propagating-house or frame, and afterwards water them very carefully and sparingly, as a rule during the early part of the day only.

CHAPTER V.

BEGONIAS AS BEDDING-PLANTS.

THOUGH so eminently valuable for the decoration of the conservatory or greenhouse, and for other similar purposes, it is as a bedding plant that the Begonia has of late years made such great and rapid strides in general popularity, and in this connection it is undoubtedly destined to be even more largely employed in the future. Even without the slightest protection the plants withstand the effects of wet and stormy weather better than anything else in cultivation, and absolutely without sustaining any injury whatever ; indeed, they really seem to enjoy a battle of this kind with the elements, that is, if the weather is mild at the time, and emerge from the contest wearing a brighter and fresher appearance than ever. At the same time, when properly established, they can endure the hottest summer ever experienced in this country without suffering much, if at all ; though in times of extreme heat and drought it is desirable to keep the roots moist and cool by means of liberal waterings, and also by placing a mulch of cocoa-nut fibre, leaf-mould, or spent hops between and around the plants.

The habit of growth, too, is at once quaint and graceful. Even the erect-flowering kinds, which are decidedly more effective and preferable for bedding purposes to the varieties with drooping blossoms, lacking the stiffness and monotony of the geranium, while all flower even more continuously and persistently the season through, and the colours are very rich, soft, and varied. As a rule, the single varieties only should be employed for bedding, for though the doubles grow and flower equally well, they do not make such an

effective display, and generally speaking the colours are not
so showy, while the blossoms being heavier are more inclined to assume the drooping position, and are thus not
seen to advantage. The type of plant with large, flat,
double or semi-double blossoms, consisting of comparatively
few well-rounded petals held well up on stiff, erect foot-
stalks, may be employed for this purpose with good effect ;
but even to these, good single kinds will be found superior.

Seedlings are very commonly employed for bedding, and with
the best results, the growth being vigorous and bushy, yet
compact, and if the seed were carefully saved from good
varieties, few of the flowers will be other than large and
fine, even when mixed or unblossomed plants are used;
while if necessary they may, of course, be selected and
marked as to colour, etc , one season for use the next. For all
work of this kind a dwarf, stiff, and branching habit, bearing an abundance of brightly-coloured flowers held erect on
stout footstalks, is of decidedly greater importance than
very large blossoms.

The method of raising the plants from seed has been
already fully described, so that it need not be repeated here.
If the seed is sown in January or the early part of February
the seedlings ought, with good culture, to be fit to plant out
about the middle of June, and they will then commence
flowering in the following month, and from about the end
of July until cut off by frost will afford a fine display of
colour.

Young seedling plants need not be placed more than 8in.
apart, with 1in. or 2in. more between the rows; indeed, if
not put out till the end of June or early part of July, even
6in. apart will suffice, especially if it is desired only to see
the flowers and mark the plants as to colour and quality for
future use. But good one-year-old tubers should be placed
10in. to 12in. apart, and large or older roots with several
stems, when grouped together in the centre of large beds or
the like, should be allowed more space still

The chief point, more particularly in dealing with small
or young plants taken from boxes, is to keep them well
watered at the roots until they have got thorough hold of
the soil and are growing freely ; if allowed to become very
or frequently dry, they will refuse to grow for some time,
and perhaps fail to make satisfactory progress for the rest

of the season. Indeed it appears to be almost impossible to give the plants too much water when growing in the open ground, and they certainly succeed better in a wet season than in a very dry one. Should they appear not to be making satisfactory progress, a thorough watering with a solution of good guano or nitrate of soda (about ¾oz. to the gallon of the latter) should be given about once a week, sprinkling the plants freely with pure water afterwards to prevent any scalding of the foliage. Towards the end of the season, however, water should be withheld, in order to enable the tubers to become thoroughly ripe and firm; an early or unexpected frost in September will also be much less injurious if the plants and soil are dry at the time than if they were in at all a wet condition.

When it is desired to obtain a batch of tubers in distinct and uniform colours, the right way to proceed is to grow the seedlings *en masse* the first year, selecting and marking them as to colour, etc., while in blossom. It is quite possible to get distinct types of plants in various colours, such as crimson, scarlet, pink, etc , to come fairly true from seed; but in order to do this the seed-bearing plants ought to be isolated in separate houses while in flower, and be carefully cross-fertilised by hand. If this is done properly quite 90 per cent. or more of the seedlings will produce flowers of the same colour as the seed-parents; but when plants of various colours are growing together the pollen gets carried by bees and other insects from one plant to another—even a puff of wind will often do it—and then the colours will get mixed. The white and yellow varieties reproduce themselves very truly from seed, especially when the plants are kept together by themselves.

After the fourth or fifth year at farthest, the tubers grow to a very large size, and produce several stems, which, moreover, grow to a considerable height, and produce comparatively small flowers, so that such plants are unsuitable for bedding, except perhaps for the centre of large beds, or for use in the second or third row of mixed borders. After a certain time it is thus better to discard them, and by raising a batch of seedlings every year, a nice, healthy young stock is easily maintained.

In the open air these Begonias are by no means particular as to soil, and will grow more or less well in any

ordinary good garden ground; but they succeed best in a
moderately light, or at any rate quite "free" and mellow
material—a nice fibrous or sandy loam is best. It can also
scarcely be made too rich by fair means, so that a dressing
of either well-decayed manure (anything at all rank or
fresh should be avoided), leaf-mould, half-decayed spent
hops (these are excellent), or a mixture of any or all these
and a little burnt earth, ought to be worked in the beds
annually a short time before planting.

I have already mentioned that small tubers of the previous season, whether they have flowered or not, make
capital bedding-plants, possessing a nice, dwarf habit, and
producing fine, large blossoms. They ought to be started
early—not later than March—so as to have time to make
a fair amount of growth before being planted out, and then
if turned out of small pots, or even transferred direct from
boxes, in June, they will begin to make a display almost
directly. The easiest and best way to start these small
tubers is in flat boxes, those about 14in. long by 10in. wide
and 2in. deep, such as are termed propagating-trays, and
are largely used by the market growers of ordinary bedding-
plants, being a very handy and useful size. Put a thin
layer of rough ashes or ballast in the bottom, with some
rough siftings, coarse leaf-mould, or spent hops over, and
then nearly fill with a light porous mixture of leaf-mould,
sand, and a little fine loam, the whole in a rather rough
state, and not pressed down too firmly. The addition of a
third or so of the whole of fresh-sifted cocoa-nut fibre is
also to be recommended, as keeping the soil thoroughly
open, and greatly assisting in the formation of roots.
Scatter a little sand over the surface, and then press the
tubers lightly into it at about 1½in. apart, and shake a
little light sandy soil or cocoa-nut fibre between the tubers,
but barely covering the crowns. The soil must be kept
hardly moist until an inch or two of growth has been made,
but sprinkle them lightly overhead on fine days; of course
the boxes must be placed in a moderately-warm house or
pit, or on a gentle hot-bed, at least until the plants are well
in growth When the leaves touch each other lift each
tuber carefully (shortly after a good watering has been
given) with plenty of earth on the roots, and transfer them
singly to 3in. or 3½in. pots, according to size, using any

good, light, loamy soil. Keep them close for a few days, until the check has been recovered, then grow on for a time in a genial temperature, harden off in May, and plant out early in June as before. Even larger or older tubers may be treated in the same way with perfect success, and indeed I have often just started them in the boxes in April, taken them out singly and carefully, with as much soil adhering as possible, and planted them out thus, in June, with excellent results, but it is better to pot them singly, if possible. When thus started in boxes, some roughish soil, consisting chiefly of leaf-mould or half-decayed spent hops, is better than a finer compost, as the plants make more and stronger roots in it, and can be taken up with quite a mass of it adhering to the latter.

Lifting and Storing the Tubers.—Directly the top growth has been cut down by the first frost in the autumn, the tubers should be lifted from the ground and removed under cover, for if the frost reaches the roots they will perish. Do not attempt to rub or wash all the soil off them at present, especially if the latter is damp, or of a stiff or adhesive nature; for if this is done the skin, which at this stage is extremely tender, will most likely come away too, and the tubers be thus injured. Lift them with a trowel, removing any loose earth, and lay them out thinly in shallow boxes, or on the floor of any dry shed or loft, for a week or two, and when moderately dry and the skin of the tubers is "set," they may be thoroughly cleaned and stored away in boxes or large pots, a few handfuls of cocoa-nut fibre being placed among them to prevent bruising, as well as to keep them from becoming unduly dry. The tubers must be kept where no frost can reach them, but as long as that is ensured, the cooler they are the better, a high temperature, especially if accompanied by a dry atmosphere, causing them to become limp and shrivelled, and this seriously injures their vitality. A range from 40deg. to 45deg. is ample at any time, and decidedly better than a higher one. Excessive damp must also be carefully guarded against.

Where the soil is light and well drained, and correspondingly dry and warm, the tubers may often be allowed to remain in the ground through the winter, and unless this

c

is unusually severe they will survive and reappear in due course the following summer. But even in the warmest parts of the country it is advisable to cover each with a spadeful of dry ashes before the winter sets in. Curiously enough, such roots as have thus been wintered in the open ground invariably start away and grow with exceptional vigour the following season, and from this fact an obvious lesson, which ought not to be neglected, may be learnt, viz., that the tubers retain the greatest amount of vitality when kept *cool* and moderately *moist* during the resting season, the soil at the depth of a few inches being, of course, never actually dry at any time during the winter.

Except in the warmest districts, however, this plan must not be depended upon too much or too often, and a choice lot of bulbs ought to be lifted in the autumn and stored under cover in the manner already described. It should also be borne in mind that in a backward season roots left in the ground will be so late in starting that the summer will be considerably advanced before the plants begin flowering. So that on the whole, and as a general rule, the best and safest way is to lift the tubers, start them in a gentle warmth in the spring, and plant them out again, annually.

One more hint: It is not uncommon for one or two sharp frosts to occur in September or the early part of October, and for a period of fine, mild, and open weather to then succeed and often last for several weeks. If, then, the beds of Begonias can be protected in some way from the effects of such early frosts for a night or two their beauty will be greatly prolonged. This is easily effected by throwing some dry litter or fern over the plants, or by stretching some thin canvas or the like over the beds.

CHAPTER VI.

DOUBLE FLOWERING VARIETIES.

THE improvement that has been effected in the double-flowering class of Begonias, and more particularly in the form and colour of the flowers and habit of the plant, is even greater than that observable in the single forms. The old doubles were poor, weedy, long-legged things with narrow-pointed leaves and comparatively shapeless flowers, composed of a multitude of small and narrow petals Now we have dwarf, sturdy plants of which the foliage can scarcely be distinguished from that of the best single kinds; but the chief improvement is to be found in the form of the blossoms, which now consist, for the most part, of a comparatively few broad and well-rounded petals, and in many instances bear a considerable resemblance, as regards build, to those of the camellia or gardenia, or in some instances to the flowers of a well-formed rose. The foot-stalks being also exceedingly stout, and the flowers not nearly so heavy as those of the older varieties, these, in many of the best new kinds, are carried quite erect, and have in consequence a very beautiful effect. Again, the colours in most of the modern kinds are exceedingly rich and varied, many exquisite shades of orange, buff, salmon, apricot, etc, as well as the ordinary white, rose, pink, scarlet, crimson, yellow, etc, being now found among these charming subjects. A really fine type of the modern erect-flowering double Begonia is indeed as choice and beautiful a flower as any conservatory can contain, and their value is considerably enhanced by the fact that the flowers last in beauty for a considerable time, especially when they are kept in a moderately cool and airy atmosphere, and carefully, yet lightly, shaded from sun From the time a good blossom fairly begins to expand until it fades is under such circumstances frequently a month, and sometimes this period is exceeded by a week or even two.

The strain on the plant occasioned by the formation of even a few of the comparatively full and heavy blossoms is, however, much greater than in the case of the single kinds, so that the plants do not, as a rule, remain in flower so continuously and persistently as the single forms; they also require somewhat more generous treatment in the way of liquid and other manures and stimulants. But this must not be overdone in any way, nor begun until the plants are in full growth and in, or coming into, flower.

On the whole the double varieties need very similar treatment to that proper for the singles, the chief difference being that as the roots are of a somewhat finer nature, the soil also ought to be of a rather finer and more sandy description, while it may also be compressed somewhat more firmly together. Free drainage must be provided, as when in full growth and flower, water must be given abundantly, but as a rule none should be afforded until the soil becomes partly dry again.

It must be admitted that the new dwarf types of erect-flowering double Begonias do not grow with nearly the same freedom as the old or inferior types, and to do them really well special care and treatment throughout is necessary. The tubers should, if possible, be started in a gentle bottom-heat, so as to promote the formation of roots as freely as possible. The soil should be thoroughly sweet and porous, yet fine rather than coarse in texture, and when in growth the plants must be very carefully potted on into larger sizes as required, never giving a shift until the last pot is pretty well filled with roots It is also an excellent plan to administer a dose or two of some mild stimulant, such as weak guano water, or a solution of sulphate of ammonia or nitrate of soda, of a strength not exceeding half-an-ounce to the gallon, less rather than more, shortly before re-potting This sets the roots actively at work, and they strike out into the fresh material directly.

The double varieties do not require such large pots as the single kinds, or even as the old-fashioned drooping-flowered sorts, the 6in. or 7in. sizes being usually sufficiently large for even two-year-old or three-year-old tubers. Instead, the vigour of the plants should be maintained by careful feeding, which may be commenced as soon as the pots are full of roots and the first flowers begin to expand. In all cases bear in mind that stimulants should be given weak and often, and that the (liquid) manure ought to be varied as much as possible.

Double Begonias are also quite as easily raised from seed as the singles, and in practice I find them even less troublesome of management, as the young plants being of a more " wiry " nature are less liable to damp off; they also commence to flower at an earlier stage than the single kinds. But however carefully the seed has been saved, only a certain percentage can be expected to produce perfectly double flowers, the rest proving either single or semi-double only. I have several times had 80 or even 90 per cent. of doubles (more or less good) in a batch; but in a general way 60 or 70 per cent. is nearer the mark, as a result of the ordinary seed of commerce, and anything over 50 per cent. must be considered good. Oddly enough, the plants that produce the single and semi-double blossoms always grow faster and more strongly than the others, and generally expand first, so do not be disheartened if the first few seedlings in a batch prove inferior or worthless, for in all probability the later ones will turn out all right; and in this respect the same rule applies to both the double and single varieties, viz., that the best flowers almost invariably appear among the later and (apparently, or at first) weaker seedlings, which ought therefore to be treated with the greatest care throughout.

As bedding plants, the double flowered kinds are, speaking generally, inferior to the single varieties, as the flowers, though individually very beautiful, are not so showy in the mass, nor are they produced so freely or continuously. Still, good double-flowering kinds, and those with erect blossoms more particularly, are very pretty and attractive for small beds, and when planted out in a nice free soil they grow and flower even better than in pots, unless, perhaps, under the most skilful treatment. A very lightly-shaded position appears to suit them best, as where protected by lofty trees at a little distance, or the like, from the rays of the midday sun only. In a pure atmosphere even the finest named doubles, as well as seedlings, succeed admirably in this way, but wherever the air is even slightly laden with smoke they should be kept entirely under glass, yet with abundant ventilation in anything like fine, warm weather

An excellent way to obtain extra fine flowers of either double or single Begonias, from small or young plants particularly, is to plant them out in a bed of specially prepared soil in a low pit or rough wooden frame, when with a little care in ventilation and shading they will grow much more strongly than in pots, and produce exceedingly fine flowers.

Double Begonias are also propagated with comparative ease by means of cuttings, and the plants being as a rule of a more wiry and bushy habit of growth than the finest single kinds, they succeed in this way, on the whole, much better than the latter, and many varieties may be increased by this method for some years with little or no perceptible deterioration. It is of course by means of cuttings that all the named doubles are propagated, and some of these have been thus increased to a very considerable extent. When the cuttings are rooted early in the season, they soon commence to flower and make very neat and pretty decorative plants in small pots during the latter part of the summer and early autumn of the same year.

The yellow varieties with double flowers are the most difficult of all to manage, having for the most part decidedly delicate constitutions, so that they must have the greatest care in all stages, the best of compost, etc.; but it is a great mistake to "coddle" even these too much, and once started they grow far better with plenty of air, certainly whenever this is reasonably pure, than if kept in a too warm and close house or pit.

Inexperienced amateurs should remember that in the double-flowering varieties it is the male or barren blossoms only that consist of more than the normal number of petals (four), the female or seed-bearing blossoms never having more than five. Unless it is desired to save seed (and bear in mind that nothing exhausts a plant or checks its flowering propensities more than the production of even a few seed-pods) it is better to pinch off all these single and ineffective female flowers as soon as or before they expand, and thereby strengthen the others

Strange and almost incredible as it may appear, the fine erect-flowering double Begonias of the present day have been obtained from the old-fashioned drooping-flowered and straggling-habited kinds, entirely by selection, and by saving seed year after year from those that evinced the most dwarf and stiff character of growth, combined with short and stout flower-stalks. Some of the first varieties to exhibit these characteristics in a marked degree were Mme. Arnoult and Suzanna Hachette. Many of the best doubles now in cultivation may be grown without any sticks or support whatever, though it must be understood that the very large and full blossoms are too heavy for even the stoutest stalks to carry without assistance, even though the habit may be naturally erect; but though individually very beautiful, these are inferior in effectiveness for almost any purpose to such varieties as, having comparatively light or less heavy and full flowers, are able to hold these in a more or less upright position. The manner in which the plants are grown also makes some considerable difference in the growth; if kept near the glass, with abundance of light and air, this will be much more dwarf and stiff than under the opposite conditions; while when grown altogether in the open these qualities will be still more conspicuous.

CHAPTER VII.

GROWING FOR EXHIBITION.

THE chief points of difference between the ordinary culture of this, or any other plant, and growing it for exhibition purposes, are, in the first place, that it is obviously useless to start with any but the very best varieties procurable—either really good and comparatively new named kinds, or carefully-selected seedlings from a superior strain —and secondly, that instead of being allowed to "rough it" at all, the very best of compost, etc., must be employed, and that regular and careful attention must be bestowed on the plants throughout. The quality of the water used for the plants also has a considerable effect upon the health and vigour of Begonias; pure rain-water is decidedly superior to anything else, though a slight trace of soot dissolved in it will be found beneficial rather than otherwise; but it should not be stored in zinc tanks, for water that has been in contact with this material for any length of time checks the free growth of these plants appreciably. River or pond water is the next best thing; but well or spring water should be avoided as being decidedly deleterious If at any time such should have to be employed, it ought to be pumped into large shallow tanks, and fully exposed to the sun for some days before being used. The addition of a small quantity of soda will render it much softer and better, or the preparation known as anticalcaire will be found even more effectual; but when either of these agents is used, the sediment that will be found at the bottom must be carefully avoided. Even when water from the mains is employed, it is advisable, if possible, to expose it to the action of the sun and air for some time, though as it has already stood in open reservoir for a considerable period, as well as been carefully filtered, it is far more suitable for any garden purposes, even when drawn straight from the tap, than well or spring water.

When growing for exhibition (unless extra large specimens are required, when three or four year-old roots are most suitable), it is best to start with carefully-selected seedling tubers that were raised and flowered in the open ground the previous season. Such tubers are invariably more sound and vigorous than those grown in pots; they will start away very strongly the following spring, and with careful culture will make very handsome plants; while if they consist of the pick of a really good batch of seedlings the flowers will prove fully equal in size and quality to the finest named varieties. These last may of course be employed, but in dealing with them it should be borne in mind that it is scarcely possible to grow the very small tubers, obtained from cuttings struck the previous autumn, that are very commonly sent out by nurserymen, into good plants of exhibition size and quality in the course of a single season Unless, therefore, good-sized tubers (named) can be obtained, the plants should be purchased a year beforehand, and grown on for a season either in pots or, preferably, planted out. It is in all cases of the greatest importance that the tubers be thoroughly matured during the previous autumn by free exposure to fresh air and sunshine, and also by gradually withholding water. If grown in pots there is nothing like turning the plants out into the open air in August and allowing them to remain exposed throughout September. But named varieties, of the single flowering kinds especially, being of course struck from cuttings, seldom, if ever, make such bushy and many-flowered specimens as good seedlings; and even if the flowers of the latter are not quite of such large size or perfect form, the plants will usually win the day against the comparatively bare and lanky examples from cuttings.

Start the tubers, if possible, in a gentle bottom-heat, and encourage the abundant formation of healthy roots by every possible means. Pot them on very carefully directly the roots begin to work freely round the sides of the first pots, but, especially in dealing with the double varieties, avoid anything like over-potting Few of the finest double varieties require larger than 6in. pots the second or even third season, and, unless very large specimens are wanted, the 8in. or 8½in. sizes afford ample room for the singles.

Keep the plants as near as possible to the glass throughout, with free ventilation, so as to solidify the growth, and large specimens must have plenty of room in order to become properly developed. Tie the shoots out carefully but not tightly to neat sticks as they advance. Shading must be given when really necessary, but not at other times. Unless the sun is actually shining strongly the plants ought to be fully exposed to the light, so that when growing for exhibition, in particular, a movable blind should always be employed.

Timing the plants is a point that must not be overlooked. Some considerable amount of experience and foresight is necessary to get the plants all just at their best by the date of the show; however fine they might be at another time, if they are not then quite sufficiently advanced, or are getting a little over, a lot of care and labour will have been thrown away. The finest flowers are produced just as the plants begin to fill their flowering-pots with roots, and after a few doses of weak stimulant have been administered. The growth of the tubers can of course be retarded in the spring by keeping them in a cool place; while, on the other hand, they may be started at any time after the end of January by subjecting them to a moderate degree of heat. Should the show be early, it will be found better to keep the plants in comparatively small pots, maintaining the vigour by means of frequent doses of weak stimulant, than to shift them on too near the time; but if late, it will be advisable to pot them on and encourage growth rather than the production of flowers during the early part of the season. When the flowers appear much before they are wanted, it is a good plan to pick off the early buds for a time, and so avoid any risk of exhausting the plants. This is specially important in the case of the double varieties.

When preparing the plants to go to the show it is necessary—at least if they have to travel any distance, or to be even slightly shaken—to tie up all the flower stems to neat sticks, for otherwise a good many of the blossoms will probably drop; in any case, the constant shaking occasioned by a journey of any extent by road will cause even the most erect and stiffest flowers to become displaced if not supported. This tying must be done with the greatest care, placing a tiny wisp of wadding round the stem beneath each tie, so as to prevent its being either cut by the latter or bruised against the stick. A tie should also be placed just below each expanded blossom, in order to prevent its snapping off at the base of the pedicel, where the joint is situated; but this must be done with great care, using plenty of wadding, and taking care not to injure the stalk or crush the flowers against the stick. In the case of plants with erect flowers, the sticks should be cut off just below each flower. The plants having arrived at their destination and been duly staged, some of the more unsightly ties and sticks may be removed, especially from the plants with more or less drooping flowers; plants trussed up tightly have a very unnatural and objectionable appearance.

It is at all times advisable, if possible, to remove the plants to the place of exhibition in the evening, as towards the close of the day the single flowers at any rate close up to a considerable extent, and are thus less liable to injury; and after a cool night in the tent or hall the plants will produce a much better and fresher appearance in the morning than if they had only just been staged after a long journey. This advice applies more particularly in hot weather.

The manner in which the single Begonias close their blossoms daily is a somewhat curious feature; it begins usually about noon, or shortly after, and the flowers close, and in some cases droop also, more and more as the afternoon passes, until towards midnight; but in the early morning they will be found all expanded and erect again, and fresher and brighter than at any other time of the day. It is also remarkable that this closing and expanding is by no means regular, and varies apparently with the weather or meteorological conditions of some kind, for some days they will begin closing much earlier than on others, while even in the morning they will sometimes expand much more fully than at other times, and occasionally, especially towards the autumn, the flowers never seem to open properly all day, while the next they will "stick up" and expand perfectly. I have sometimes tried to trace some correspondence between these erratic movements and that of the barometer or weather prospects, but without any definite result so far ; but if investigations were undertaken systematically by an expert meteorologist they might possibly lead to something.

Dropping of the Blossoms.—This failing is at times very troublesome among Begonias, and it undoubtedly constitutes a slight disadvantage, particularly under certain circumstances It may arise from any one of several distinct causes, but is sometimes inherent in the plant, which ought then to be discarded. Irregular or injudicious watering is a frequent cause of the flowers dropping prematurely, and neglect of any kind will often have the same effect. A sudden change in the weather frequently causes the flowers to drop wholesale, and if the house is shut up, or if when already closed it is too suddenly opened, the same thing may occur. In large towns, where the atmosphere is heavily laden with smoke, dropping is more troublesome than out in the pure air of the country ; indeed, in very smoky localities the plants are scarcely worth cultivating, as it is difficult at times to get a fully-expanded flower at all. But under ordinary conditions a plant that persistently drops its flowers prematurely should be thrown away as useless.

Begonias as Basket Plants.—As basket plants, either for conservatory decoration or for use in the open air, in a position not too fully exposed to the sun, the tuberous Begonias are unsurpassed Both single and double flowered kinds are suitable for this purpose, but only varieties of a drooping habit should be chosen. Either named kinds or seedlings may be employed in this way, and any good nurseryman would be able to supply a collection specially adapted for this purpose

The tubers should be started in small pots, and if the baskets are large the plants should be shifted into 5in. pots when more root-room is required. Plants with three or four stems are best, so that unless varieties of a naturally branching habit can be had, the tubers should be not less than two or three years of age. Line the baskets well with long soft moss, such as sphagnum, and fill up with a compost of fresh turfy loam, leaf-mould, and sand, placing the plant in the centre of each, and making all firm. Small pieces of the variegated *Tradescantia zebrina*, of *Isolepis gracilis*, or a few trailing lobelias or thunbergias may be planted round the edge so as to hang over and improve the effect. Water carefully at first, but abundantly as soon as the plants are established, especially in hot weather. Should the soil become very dry at any time the basket may be dipped in a tub or tank for half-an-hour with benefit.

Insects and Diseases.—Begonias are fortunately liable to the attacks of but few insects, and as far as I am aware to only one kind of disease. Green-fly (aphides) will sometimes attack the young leaves or shoots; but this seldom occurs unless the atmosphere is allowed to become too dry or the plants are neglected in some way. Healthy and vigorous examples are seldom affected. When, however, these insects do settle in the points of the shoots, the effect is quickly observed in the leaves becoming curled and stunted A gentle fumigation with tobacco is the best remedy; but if this is given after the flowers expand, it will cause them to become discoloured at the edges. Good culture is the best preventive of insects of all kinds. Thrips and red spider occasionally appear in the under-sides of the leaves, but only when the plants have been grossly neglected or stand directly over hot pipes or a flue. I have never known plants in the open air to be affected by insects of any kind, and hardly ever by disease. The only disease to which they are liable is of a fungoid nature—a kind of rust, in fact. It appears on the under-sides of the leaves and on the stems, and in a short time completely checks the growth and renders the whole plant very brittle. It is almost invariably caused by neglect, by a parched atmosphere, or by want of fresh air. In the earlier stages it may be got rid of by the use of a preparation of sulphur, or sulphide of potassium is even more effectual; but the best plan is to turn out any affected plants into the open air (in summer only, of course), preferring a lightly-shaded spot, and keeping the soil evenly moist. As a rule, they will soon start into a healthy growth again from the base, when the worst parts may be cut away, and all will go well subsequently

In very hot and bright weather plants under glass will sometimes "go off" in a somewhat unaccountable manner, especially when standing on high shelves near the glass, and only lightly shaded. This is not a disease, but a kind of collapse due to the excessive heat causing too rapid transpiration. Let the plants be carefully and regularly watered, and rather freely ventilated, especially at night, and with a moderately heavy shade they will be all right. Newly-potted plants are more liable to be thus affected than others.

CHAPTER VIII.

HYBRIDISING AND SEED-SAVING.

IT is simply by persistently selecting the finest flowers, and sowing seed from them year after year, that the wonderful improvements in Begonias already described have been effected. Fortunately the plants seed freely, and if the seed is carefully gathered when ripe, and duly sown, many of the seedlings will prove equal in quality to the parent plant or plants, and few probably superior in some respects if not in all. By saving and sowing the seed annually from these improved forms, a sure if not very rapid gain, not only in the size of the flowers, but in their colour, form, and substance, as well as in the habit of the plant is effected

Anyone may save seed from one or more good single or double Begonias, but it will be evident to all that it is a mere waste of time and labour to take seed from any but really first-class varieties. If good, sound seed that will germinate freely and do well is to be obtained, it is, however, necessary that the pods shall have been fertilised by the contact of pollen, from a male or barren flower, with the group of corkscrew-like processes in the centre of the female blossom, which constitutes the stigma. A female Begonia flower may be fertilised with pollen from a male flower on either the same plant or another one, but as a general rule it is decidedly preferable to employ pollen from another example, even if of the same colour. Unless fertilisation has thoroughly taken place, or, in other words, unless the seed has been properly impregnated, either the pod will drop before it ripens, or the seed will germinate imperfectly or not at all

Fertilisation take place in one of two ways, viz., naturally or by artificial means. Thus, in the summer-time the pollen is frequently carried by bees and other insects from flower to flower, and in a light and airy house, especially in bright and dry weather, the atmosphere will at times be full of pollen; some of this will probably settle on the stigmas of the blossoms, which thus become impregnated, and fertile seed result. It is, however, worthy of note that while the commoner varieties, and the old-fashioned single kinds in particular, seed freely and almost spontaneously, the choicer and more modern varieties are comparatively shy of producing seed, and need to be specially grown in a light, airy, and moderately sunny structure, and to be carefully fertilised by hand. Again, seed saved from flowers that have been fertilised naturally, or by chance, is never to be depended upon, and, as a rule, should not be made use of. If the house contains nothing but first-rate varieties, it may be employed on a pinch, and may turn out fairly well; but as a large pro-portion will probably be self-fertilised, that is, impregnated with pollen from the same plant, much cannot be expected of it.

Hybridising (cross-fertilisation) is a term applied to the process of transferring the pollen of one plant to the female or seed-flowers of another one, and it is in this way that the best results are almost invariably obtained This may be done directly, by gathering the male flower and applying the mass of pollen-bearing anthers in its centre to the stigma of the female flower, or, *secundum artem*, by employ-ing a soft camel-hair brush with which to transfer the pollen. Personally, I much prefer the first method, as being at once less troublesome and more effectual. The best time to perform this operation is during the middle of the day, say, from 11 a.m. to 2 p.m. or 3 p.m., but pre-ferring the forenoon, and choosing, if possible, bright dry weather with the sun shining at the time. The atmosphere of the house, as well as the plants themselves, ought to be moderately dry, as the pollen is then liberated more freely and fertilisation more readily accomplished; and the more the plants have been "hardened" by being exposed to abundance of fresh air and only lightly shaded for some time previously the better.

When mixed hybrid seed is required, a common plan is to fertilise the blossoms on a number of plants promiscuously with pollen gathered haphazard on a rather large brush or pencil, and this method is generally employed by those who grow the seed in quantity for sale. But when making particular " crosses " with a definite aim, the pollen of the one parent plant must be transferred directly to the flowers of the other by one of the means above referred to. The flowers or pods so operated upon may be marked by tying bits of various coloured silk or cotton round the footstalk, and the particulars should then be entered in a note-book. It is in this way that new tints or shades are obtained. The beautiful orange, salmon, and apricot-coloured flowers, of which we have now so many, have been obtained, for instance, by crossing varieties with yellow blossoms with pollen from those of various shades of red or pink, and *vice versâ*, and by this method new or more intense and brilliant colours, as well as different forms and types of the flower, are constantly being raised. Again, by crossing a plant with well-formed blossoms, having wide and nicely-rounded petals, but small, with another possessing less compact and shapely, but considerably larger, flowers of the same colour, one or more plants combining the size of the one with the fine form and good colour of the other will probably be obtained, and so on, *ad infinitum*. The possibilities that the field of skilful hybridising opens up are, indeed, endless, and each success is only the stepping-stone to future endeavour and accomplishment.

Supposing, however, the object is to secure seed that will produce plants of any particular colour, and as true as possible to the parents, then we select for the seed-parents two plants with flowers of the desired shade, and as nearly alike as possible, and cross them to and fro between themselves only. If, now, the type is a fairly distinct one (this is an important point), and the plants can be isolated so as to prevent any possibility of pollen from any flowers of another colour coming in contact with them, the resulting seedlings will probably come true to colour to the extent of 90 per cent. or more ; indeed, I have seen a bed containing several thousands of seedlings from a crimson-flowered bedding variety with not 1 per cent. of " rogues " among them, the only difference being that the seedlings

D

from one plant or cross were just about a shade darker than
those from the other. But seeds saved in a house containing a mixed collection will be almost certain to produce
plants varying considerably in colour, even if taken carefully from distinct plants.

But when raised from good hybridised seed these
Begonias are liable to "sport" or develop fresh breaks
occasionally in a remarkable manner. Here and there
among a batch of seedlings will be found a plant entirely
different from any of those from which seed was saved, and
often with far larger and finer flowers than any of the
parents. In this way some of the greatest strides have
been made, and it is to a great extent this feature that
renders the occupation so interesting, and, indeed, absorbing.
The same "break," or a very similar one, will also often occur
in two or more places at or about the same time. I have
known this to occur on several occasions. It stands to
reason that the larger the number of seedlings one has to
select from, the greater the chance of obtaining an advance
on existing varieties; and it is in this way that the large
Begonia growers have been able to progress as they have
done. The man who grows a thousand seedlings has ten
times the chance of securing a really novel and improved
variety than one who cultivates a hundred possesses, and
one who raises ten thousand ten times more again.

It may be as well here to briefly describe the *modus
operandi* of such growers as Messrs. Blackmore & Langdon,
Cannell, Laing, Davis, and Ware, who grow something like
a quarter to in some cases nearly half a million Begonias,
chiefly from seed, annually. The seed (carefully saved
in distinct colours and kinds for various purposes) is sown
early in the year, and the young plants are treated as
described in the chapter on propagation, pp. 21 to 25,
the greater part being pricked out into shallow boxes,
hardened off in May, and planted out in well-prepared
beds in June or the early part of July. Nearly all
will flower during August and September, and they are
then gone over by expert men, and carefully marked as
to colour and quality. During the following winter and
spring the tubers that have produced the worst flowers are
disposed of at a low price as "Mixed Begonias" for
bedding, the next best being marked to colour for the same

purpose in two or three qualities; then other and better classes for pot-culture are formed at still higher prices, and a few dozens of the very best are retained and grown in pots for show and exhibition the following season. These are also usually "named" and propagated by means of cuttings, while seed is also saved from them for future use.

In saving seed from the double-flowered kinds, a plant with perfectly double blossoms of the finest quality is invariably selected for the seed parent; but as these fully double flowers afford no pollen, recourse must be had to those with semi-double flowers only, and the more nearly double they are the better, naturally. Some varieties that when well grown produce perfectly double blossoms, throw semi-double ones if judiciously "starved" (*i.e*, kept rather short of water, and allowed no manure of any kind, for a time), and if pollen from such can be had, a larger percentage of double flowers among the seedlings will result. From seed saved with extra care I have frequently had 90 per cent. of double flowers, more or less good; but in a general way anything over 50 per cent. may be reckoned a good result. I have never been able to obtain such good results, either in germinating power or in quality, from bought seed (single or double) as from that of my own saving; but I may perhaps be allowed to say that by far the best Begonia seed, double especially, I have ever obtained was from Mr. J. R. Box, of Croydon; both in quality and germinating power nothing better could be desired.

At one time the continental raisers were decidedly ahead of us in the excellence of the Begonias raised and sent out. But the English growers soon surpassed them, first in the single-flowered kinds, and since as regards the double ones; and now we are ahead of the world in both classes.

CHAPTER IX.

SELECTION OF TUBEROUS-ROOTED VARIETIES.

THE following varieties constitute the cream of the named kinds of tuberous-rooted Begonias at present in cultivation, and may be depended upon either for exhibition or for ordinary decorative purposes. The name given in brackets after each is that of the raiser.

SINGLE VARIETIES.

ADMIRATION.—Flowers of vivid orange-scarlet. A free flowering begonia of dwarf compact habit. See Fig. 1, p 53.

ALBA FIMBRIATA (Ware).—A fine, large pure white flower, with fringed petals.

ALBA ROSEA (Laing).—Rosy-pink, with white centre; very free-flowering.

ALICE MANNING.—Primrose-yellow blossoms in masses; very effective.

BEXLEY WHITE (Ware).—An immense flower of the purest white.

BLACK KNIGHT (Ware).—Deep rich crimson.

CHALLENGER (Ware).—Dark crimson fine form, very free.

COL. KIDD (Cannell).—Deep red, massive flowers.

COUNTESS NELSON (Laing).—A charming blush-coloured flower, extra fine.

DEAN SWIFT (Ware).—A beautifully-formed flower of a soft salmon-red hue.

DUCHESS OF LEINSTER (Laing).—Orange-buff, large erect flowers.

DUKE OF RICHMOND AND GORDON (Laing).—A very fine dark crimson; superb.

EARL GROSVENOR (Cannell).—Orange-scarlet, very large.

EARL OF ESSEX (Laing).—Orange-scarlet, extra fine.

GARONNE (Ware).—Dark bronze, a beautiful colour.

Part of Messrs. Blackmore & Langdon's Group of Tuberous Begonias awarded Silver Cup at Holland Park.

GIGANTEA (Laing).—Rose-pink, light centre; extra large, and of fine form.

GOLIATH (Ware).—Golden-bronze, lighter margin; large and fine.

FIG. 1.   ADMIRATION.

J. W. WILKINSON (Laing).—Vivid scarlet.

LADY GRIMTHORPE (Laing.)—Rose colour; extra large and fine; new.

LADY MARY LLOYD (Laing).—Salmon; a splendid variety.

FIG 2. QUEEN OF WHITES.

LADY PIGOTT (Laing) —Large erect salmon-coloured blossoms.

LADY PLOWDEN.—Pure white, superb.

LADY WILKINS.—Golden bronze, with large and well-formed blossoms.

LORD BYRON (Ware).—Brilliant scarlet, with white centre ; very effective.

LORD MAYOR (Laing).—Rich rose ; free.

MARGINATA (Ware) —Large round flowers, with very thick petals ; colour, pure white with a margin of bright pink ; a very striking flower

MARQUIS OF BRISTOL —Light yellow.

MISS A. DE ROTHSCHILD (Laing).—Pure yellow ; superb flower.

MISS AGNES STEWART (Cannell).—Soft yellow, with pink edge ; very pretty

MISS MABEL COOPER (Ware).—Salmon-rose ; bright and attractive.

MONARCH (Ware).—Rich crimson, bold flowers.

MORAVIA (Ware).—Deep scarlet ; very fine.

MR. W. MILLER (Laing).—Dark crimson, extra.

MRS. FARINI.—Salmon-red ; very full and floriferous.

MRS. J. CHAMBERLAIN (Laing).—White and rose, the upper part of each flower darker than the lower.

MRS. J. THORPE (Cannell).—White, the petals edged with reddish-lake.

MRS. R DEAN (Laing).—Pink, with a carmine margin ; petals beautifully crimped.

MRS. W H. FORSTER (Cannell) —Brilliant red with pure white centre ; fine

NOVELTY (Ware).—Bright magenta, with pure white centre ; new and striking.

PENSACOLA (Ware) —Rich pink, of fine form, and very free.

PRIDE OF BEXLEY (Ware).—Delicate blush, a charming flower.

QUEEN OF WHITES (Sutton and Sons).—Large, erect, pure white flowers of great substance. See Fig 2, p. 54, for which we are indebted to Messrs. Sutton and Sons, of Reading.

SIR J. B MAPLE (Laing).—A magnificent scarlet flower.

SOVEREIGN (Ware).—Rich golden-yellow, very free, and excellent in every way.

STANSTEAD SURPRISE (Laing).—Deep rose, very large.

TORBY LAING (Laing).—Reddish orange-yellow ; an unusual colour

VENUS (Ware).—Delicate pink, a most perfect flower ; vigorous and fine.

W. MARSHALL (Cannell). — Orange-buff ; very rich and charming.

DOUBLE VARIETIES.

ALBA PLENA CAMELLIÆ-FLORA.—Pure white, dwarf habit ; erect and free flowering.

ALBA PLENA FIMBRIATA.—Blush-white, beautifully fringed.

ALTHŒAFLORA (Davis).—Quite a distinct variety, resembling
a fine bloom of the double Hibiscus. In point of size this is
one of the largest Begonias ever raised; but its chief charac-
teristic is the new and distinct colour of the flower—a lovely
bright rosy-cerise shaded to rose in the centre, the extreme
edge of the petals being of a deep cerise. The flower is very
large, double, and fimbriated, a free bloomer, of compact

FIG. 3. ALTHŒAFLORA

robust habit; a great acquisition. See Fig. 3 (above), for
which we are indebted to Mr. B. R. Davis, of Yeovil.

BEAUTY OF BELGROVE (Cannell).—A large and exquisite
flower of the colour of a La France rose; extra.

B. R. DAVIS.—Crimson-scarlet, large, erect, fine.

CAMELLIA-FLORA (Davis).—A large and perfect flower of the
camellia type. In colour an extremely rich magenta-cerise,
shaded with a darker tint. A valuable variety for exhibition.

See Fig. 4, for which we are indebted to Mr. B. R. Davis, of Yeovil.

COUNTESS OF CRAVEN (Laing).—Large pure white flowers, held quite erect; dwarf habit, extra.

COUNTESS RUSSELL.—Bright, salmon camellia-shaped flowers, erect and free.

FIG. 4. CAMELLIA-FLORA.

COUNTESS OF ZETLAND (Laing).—Pure white, large erect flowers.

DANDY (Davis).—Intensely bright carmine-scarlet, extremely free flowering, and vigorous in habit; a perfect gem for the button-hole. See Fig. 5, p. 58, for which we are indebted to Mr. B. R. Davis, of Yeovil.

DIAMOND JUBILEE (Box).—A magnificent flower of a deep

yellow colour, vigorous and erect habit ; the best double
yellow yet raised. See Fig. 6, p. 59.

DUCHESS OF MARLBOROUGH.—(Laing) —Light salmon-pink,
fine form, erect habit, extra. (See Fig. 7, p. 60).

DUKE OF FIFE (Laing).—Rosy-salmon, large erect flowers ;
very free and fine.

DUKE OF GRAFTON (Laing) —Pure salmon-colour, extra large.

DUKE OF TECK (Ware).—Double crimson flowers, very large
and massive.

DUKE OF YORK (Laing).—Deep rose, lighter centre ; very large
and double, erect ; new.

FIG 5. DANDY.

E T. COOK (Laing) —Rich glowing crimson, large and very
double , one of the best in this colour.

FERONIA (Ware) —A very bright pink flower, robust habit and
erect flowering.

FIGARO (Box).—Bright orange-scarlet, fine form and habit.

FLAMINGO (Cannell).—A brilliant scarlet flower, free, and of a
capital habit.

GEN. OWEN WILLIAMS (Cannell).—Rich crimson, large erect
flowers ; dwarf habit.

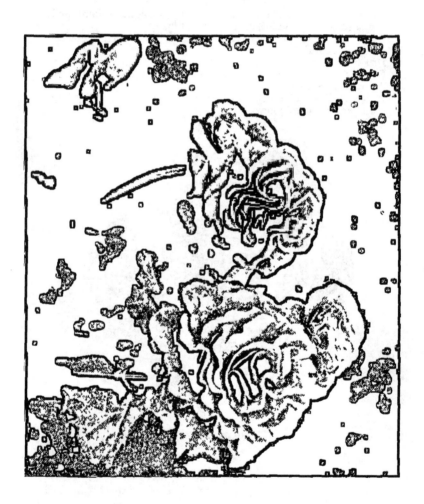

FIG 7. DUCHESS OF MARLBOROUGH.

FIG. 8. MISS GRIFFITH

FIG. 9. MISS PEREIRA.

GOLDFINCH (Box).—Bright yellow, large erect flowers, free and good,

H. M. THE DOWAGER EMPRESS FREDERICK (Laing).—Rich rosy-pink, rose-shaped blossoms, fine.

HENRI ROSAIRE (Laing).—Saffron-yellow, very large and fine flowers, extra.

HENSHAW RUSSELL (Laing).—A superb scarlet variety, and one of the best of any colour ever raised. The habit is robust

FIG 10. PICOTEE.

and dwarf, and the large and brilliantly coloured flowers stand up boldly and quite erect above the foliage. A simply grand flower.

LADY BALFOUR OF BURLEIGH (Laing).—Large yellow flowers, erect ; first class.

FIG. 11. SUTTON'S DOUBLE.

LADY DORINGTON (Laing).—Blush-pink, very beautiful, large
  erect, and camellia-shaped.
LADY DUNSANY (Laing).—A superb pink flower.
LAFAYETTE (Cannell).—Rich bright scarlet, very dwarf and
  free, with erect flowers; one of the best for bedding purposes.
LEVIATHAN.—Deep rose, very large, erect.
LOTHAIN.—A very bright crimson flower; fine.
MME. LA BARONNE DE ST. DIDIER (Cannell).—Soft delicate
  yellow; extra large and fine.
MARQUIS OF STAFFORD (Laing).—Crimson, large, fine form
  and very free.
MISS EDITH WYNNE (Cannell).—Pure creamy white, drooping,
  but very lovely; a capital kind for a basket.
MISS FALCONER (Cannell).—Clear yellow, very free and fine;
  splendid habit.
MISS GRIFFITH (Box).—Pure white, very large and full flowers,
  with beautifully frilled petals; an exquisite variety. (See
  Fig. 8, p. 61.)
MISS NORA HASTINGS (Cannell).—Delicate fawn-colour, back of
  petals rosy-salmon; fine large flowers.
MR. A. CHAMBERLAIN (Laing).—A fine scarlet variety, with
  large well-formed flowers.
MRS. CORNWALLIS WEST (Cannell).—Soft yellow, shaded
  apricot; an exquisitely beautiful flower.
MRS. FRENCH (Ware).—Creamy-white flowers of perfect form;
  very free and large.
MRS. PEREIRA (Box).—Pure white, of perfect Camellia form,
  yet large and free. Good habit. (See Fig. 9, p. 62).
MRS. REGNART (Laing).—Chrome-yellow, fine erect flowers;
  dwarf habit; petals prettily undulated.
OCTAVIE (Cannell).—An old but charming variety, with rather
  small but beautifully-formed pure white blossoms like little
  camellias. Free-branching habit and wonderfully floriferous,
  even small plants in 3in. pots flowering freely. This fine
  kind has been propagated by thousands from cuttings, which
  strike freely, but still retains its character and a considerable
  share of vigour.
PICOTEE (Davis).—Plant dwarf; the blooms of a delicate white,
  each petal having a clear and well-defined pink margin,
  sufficiently broad to make it exceedingly attractive. See
  Fig. 10, p. 63, for which we are indebted to Mr. B. R.
  Davis, of Yeovil.
PRINCESS CHRISTIAN (Laing).—Delicate primrose; a lovely
  flower of fine form and great substance.
PRINCESS MAY (Ware). — Pure white camellia-formed
  blossoms, the petals beautifully undulated or crimped at
  the edges.
QUEEN OF QUEENS (Box).—Bright orange, shaded apricot;
  splendid habit, and one of the finest ever raised.

a

ROSEBUD (Cannell).—Large camellia-shaped blossoms of exquisite form, and in colour of the most delicate pink.

ROSY MORN (Laing).—Extra large flowers of a rosy-pink tint, with broad wavy petals, distinct and fine.

SIR T. LAWRENCE (Laing).—Rich dark crimson, large erect flowers.

SNOWDRIFT (Laing).—A beautiful pure white flower, with very large camellia-shaped blossoms, and an erect and very floriferous habit.

SUTTON'S DOUBLE (Sutton).—A strain having massive double flowers of true rosette form, and, as depicted in the illustration (See Fig. 11, page 64), the flowers are borne more or less erect. The strain includes a large number of rich colours, pure white, yellow, salmon, pink, scarlet, and crimson, while well-flowered plants can be grown from seed in six months.

THOS. WHITELAW (Cannell).— Fawn, shaded buff, and edged rosy red ; very distinct and pretty.

TRIOMPHE (Ware)—Splendid rich bright crimson, immense flowers, grand habit ; one of the very best.

The Multiflora Varieties (Double-flowering).—

This comparatively new class consists of a few varieties of a very dwarf, compact, and bushy habit of growth, with medium-sized blossoms, which are very freely produced. These qualities render them exceedingly suitable for bedding purposes, and for this work I can strongly recommend them, having given them a thorough trial on a rather extensive scale.

These varieties, which, by the way, are of French origin, as the names denote, have tuberous roots, and are extremely free and robust in growth. They should be started into growth in a gentle warmth in the spring, in either small pots or boxes, and be planted out, preferably, just *before* they commence flowering, in beds of light, rich soil, and a sunny position. They are easily increased by means of cuttings taken in the spring or early summer, and also by division of the bulbs just as they are starting into growth.

The principal varieties are :—

AURORA.—A kind of soft orange or apricot colour.

EUGÉNE VERDIER.—Vermilion.

HENRY URBAN —Madder-pink.

L'AVENIR.—Reddish scarlet.

L'ENFANT TROUVÉ.—White.

LUCIE MOURY.—Rose.

LUTEA FLORE PLENO NANA —Yellow, very dwarf.

MME A. COURTOIS.—Creamy white.

MME. LOUIS URBAN.—Deep rose (Award of Merit).

MULTIFLORA GRACILIS.—Red

PETIT HENRI.—Carmine.
ROSEA MULTIFLORA.—Soft rose.
SOLEIL D'AUSTERLITZ.—Bright scarlet.
SURPASSE DAVISI.—Crimson, with bronzy foliage.

The following are more recent additions :—

[SINGLES.]

FAIRY QUEEN (Ware).—Large, substantial, rich salmon-coloured flowers.
GIPSY QUEEN (Davis).—Deep bronze. Very free, and of stiff, bushy habit.
LA FRANCE (Davis).—Bright rose-pink flowers, of good form and substance.
LITTLE DORRIT (Davis).—Pale salmon flowers, with elegantly-frilled petals.
*NIVALIS (Ware).—Rich yellow, large and handsome.
ROYALTY (Davis).—Rich crimson, with broad, smooth petals.
SNOW QUEEN (Davis).—A lovely pure white, with fimbriated petals.
*SUPERBUM (Ware).—Handsome flowers of a soft salmon.

[DOUBLES.]

ANSON (Davis).—Flowers yellow, with broad, smooth petals, margined with pink.
BRIGHTNESS (Blackmore & Langdon).—Medium-sized, shapely orange-coloured flowers.
*COUNTESS CADOGAN (Ware).—Flowers orange-yellow ; plant of bushy, free-flowering habit.
DE WET (Davis).—Handsome yellow flowers, with thick, smooth petals.
DUKE OF CONNAUGHT (Ware).—Flowers bright scarlet, borne on long, stiff stems clear of the foliage.
*EDNA MAY (Cannell).—Flowers medium to small, bright salmon, with finely crumped petals.
EXQUISITE (Cannell). — Medium-sized, shapely deep salmon flowers, shading to light pink towards the centre, the broad petals being distinctly frilled.
GLADYS HEMSLEY (Jones). — Rather small, Camellia-shaped, light pink flowers, almost white near the centre.
MASTERPIECE (Blackmore & Langdon).—Rich crimson flowers of perfect form and substance.
MISS DOROTHY HARDWICK (Blackmore & Langdon).—Lovely shell-pink, Hollyhock-shaped flowers, having frilled petals.
MR. HENRY CLARK (Ware).—Flowers bright scarlet, with frilled petals.
MR. W. G. VALENTINE (Ware).—Flowers scarlet, with broad, round, smooth petals.

E 2

MRS. ANDREW TWEEDIE (Ware). — Large white flowers, touched with green in the centre.

MRS. HALL (Laing).—Flowers salmon-pink, passing to pale pink in the raised centre.

*MRS. HORTON (Cannell).—Large, substantial, creamy-white flowers.

MRS. W. G. VALENTINE (Ware).—Flowers primrose-yellow, bold and distinct; of excellent form.

ODORATA ROSEA PLENA. — Sweet-scented, perfectly double rose-pink flowers.

PRIMA DONNA (Davis).—Flowers snow-white, of good size and shape.

PROFESSOR LANCIANA (Blackmore & Langdon). — Bright salmon flowers.

QUEEN ALEXANDRA (Ware).—Flowers pale salmon, suffused and edged with orange-scarlet. A first-rate variety.

SAMUEL POPE (Ware).—Flowers large, white, edged with rose-pink. Distinct and pretty.

S. T. WRIGHT (Ware).—Flowers apricot, touched with orange.

CHAPTER X.

OTHER SPECIES, VARIETIES, AND HYBRIDS.

As stated at the commencement of this book, the whole of the tuberous-rooted hybrid Begonias of which we have hitherto treated are the descendants of some half-dozen of the original species only. We will now proceed to consider some of the most useful, from a horticultural or decorative point of view, of the numerous other species of this wonderful and most interesting genus, with the garden varieties and hybrids that have so far been obtained from them.

These it will be most convenient to divide into four classes or sections, as follows: (1) Winter-flowering varieties with tuberous roots; (2) Winter-flowering varieties with fibrous roots; (3) "Rex" or ornamental-leaved varieties (all these have fibrous roots); and (4) Miscellaneous varieties.

Winter flowering Begonias with Tuberous Roots.—This class consists at present of a few varieties only, though it is not improbable that they may be largely added to, by hybridising, in the near future. It comprises the following three varieties: John Heal (rosy-carmine), Adonis (bright rose); Winter Gem (crimson-scarlet).

The first of these was obtained by crossing *Begonia socotrana* (a very distinct species from the island of Socotra) with B. Viscountess Doneraile (a hybrid from B. Monarch and *B. Sedeni*). It has a very dwarf habit, with a profusion of brightly-coloured flowers, produced on branched stems during the dull part of the year—from October to March, or thereabouts. A peculiarity of this kind is that all the flowers are male ones, so that no seed is produced, but the plant is easily increased by means of cuttings. Adonis is the result of a cross between a tuberous variety and John Heal; this also produces male flowers only, and is increased by means of cuttings. Winter Gem was obtained by crossing *B. socotrana* with a crimson-flowered tuberous variety; it is propagated, like *B. socotrana* itself, by means of scaly bulbils, which are formed round the base of the stem during the period of growth, these remaining dormant through the summer and being started into growth in heat in September.

B socotrana itself has nearly circular leaves, rolled back at the edges, and bright rose-coloured flowers nearly 2in. in diameter. It has semi-tuberous roots, but, like the above hybrids from it, is an uncertain subject to keep through the winter; so a young stock, obtained from cuttings, which should be taken in February or March, or from bulbils, ought always to be secured in case of the old plants being lost.

All plants of this class may be grown well in a free porous compost of fine fibrous loam, leaf-mould, and sand, with a third or fourth of peat added, unless the loam is very fibrous and mellow. They must be placed in an intermediate or mild stove temperature of 55deg. to 70deg., about the end of September, and, with plenty of light and water, as required, they will blossom freely for some months.

Winter-flowering Begonias with Fibrous Roots.

—This is a large and interesting as well as useful class, and as it is being steadily increased and improved by the introduction of new and in many cases very superior hybrid and other varieties, it will probably receive a larger share of attention in the future   Unfortunately, these winter-flowering Begonias can only be grown by those who possess a house heated to a temperature some degrees above that of an ordinary greenhouse, a range of 55degs. or 60degs. to 65degs. or 70degs, according to the weather, but never less than 50degs, being most suitable. The cuttings may be struck in February, March, or even as late as April, if comparatively small plants are only needed. Cut them just below the third or fourth joints, and insert them singly in small pots of very sandy peat (or a mixture of equal parts of loam, leaf-mould, cocoa-nut fibre, and sand will answer equally well), surfacing the pots in either case with nearly an inch of pure sand. They will root readily in a hot-bed frame, or in any warm house or pit, with a bottom heat of 70degs. to 75degs., or even without this aid if they can be kept moderately close and shaded from the sun. When rooted, harden them a little, and then shift first into 4in. pots and afterwards into those 6in. or 7in. across, in which they will flower freely; though, if preferred, larger specimens still may be obtained by potting them on into 9in. to 12in. sizes not later than July.

A very suitable compost consists of two parts of good fibrous or turfy loam, one part of sandy peat, one part of leaf-mould, plenty of sharp or coarse sand, a little fine " ballast " (burnt earth) or bricks broken small, and a dash each of soot and some good fertiliser, such as Thomson's. The plants may, however, be grown without any peat if more convenient, or in peat and sand with a little leaf-mould only, but on the whole the compost described is to be preferred. Keep them in genial growing temperature throughout the summer, with a moderately moist atmosphere, though they do not require or enjoy the amount of humidity that many stove plants demand. From the middle or end of May to the middle of September little or no artificial warmth is really necessary, the sun's heat being made the most of by closing the house or pit a couple of hours before the sun goes off it, and leaving the ventilators closed until the structure has again become thoroughly warmed through in the morning. Light shade from all strong sun should be given, but do not overdo it in any way. Ventilate freely in all fine and warm weather, so as to secure sturdy plants and substantial growth. Towards the end of September remove the plants to their winter quarters, taking care that they do not sustain any check from an unduly low temperature at any time. If they are to flower freely and continuously, they must be kept near the glass, in full light, and unshaded by creepers or other tall plants growing over or too near them.

In the spring the plants should be hardened off a little so as to secure substantial cuttings, and when a sufficient number of these have been taken and are seen to be doing well, the old plants had better be thrown away, as the young stock will succeed much better, make neater and prettier specimens, and may be grown to any reasonable size by the autumn, if rooted in February or March. Some of the newer hybrid kinds, such as Gloire de Sceaux, Triomphe de Lemoine, and Gloire de Lorraine, are exceedingly beautiful objects when seen in good condition.

The following are the best and most useful of this class :—

BRUANTI ROSEA FLORIBUNDA. — A beautiful rose-coloured variety.

CARRIERI (Cannell).—A pure white variety, remarkably free, and of a robust and vigorous habit, seldom failing to do well.

CINNABARINA.—A tall, vigorous kind, with orange-coloured blossoms ; almost a perpetual flowerer.

CORBEILLE DE FEU.—Bright coral-red : dwarf and free.

DIGSWELLIENSIS.—Soft pink ; very pretty. compact habit.

DIPETALA.—Pink ; very fine.

DUCHARTREI (Early).—White ; very free ; rather tall in growth ; foliage of *B. Scharffiana.*

DUCHESS OF YORK (Sutton and Sons).—A new and charming variety, with flowers of a delicate carmine colour, which are considerably larger than those of the ordinary begonia superflorens. See Fig. 12, p. 73, for which we are indebted to Messrs. Sutton and Sons, of Reading.

FUCHSIOIDES (syn. *B. miniata*).—Drooping flowers of a bright coral-red colour, in clusters : very useful

GERBE FLEURIE.—A hybrid from *B. semperflorens*, with light rosy flowers ; erect habit.

GLOIRE DE LORRAINE (Rothschild). — Rosy-carmine flowers , very free, dwarf habit ; extra fine.

GLOIRE DE SCEAUX (Rothschild). — A magnificent variety, with large well-opened flowers of a silky pink, held quite erect just above the foliage, which, being of a rich bronzy colour, is also very ornamental. In beauty, this is almost equal to many of the tuberous-rooted kinds.

GRIFFITHI.—White blossoms ; distinct.

HYBRIDA FLORIBUNDA (syn. *Multiflora*) — Bright coral coloured blossoms ; extremely pretty and free

HYDROCOTYLIFOLIA.—Bronzy foliage ; flowers all through the winter.

INGRAMI (syn. *B. Saundersoni*).—Reddish-pink ; deep green foliage ; dwarf.

INSIGNIS (syn. *B. incarnata*).—Lilac-pink ; an old but vigorous and useful variety.

KNOWSLEYANA.—Bears silvery-blush flowers in great abundance; vigorous growth, and fine for cutting.
LUCIDA COCCINEA.—Pale scarlet flowers.

FIG. 12. DUCHESS OF YORK.

MANICATA.—A strong-growing kind, with large leaves, and
dense heads of delicate pink blossoms.
MONS. HARDY.—Light rose colour.
MOONLIGHT.—Has large flowers of the purest white.

NITIDA (syn. *B. obliqua*).—Silvery-blush flowers, and large
   deep green, shiny foliage.
NITIDA ALBA.—Pure white; otherwise similar to the foregoing.
PRES BOUREILLES.—Fine silvery-pink flowers and handsome
   foliage
READING SNOWFLAKE.—An improved form of *B. semperflorens*
   (white), the blossoms being quite twice the size of those of
   the latter.   There are also a considerable number of sub-
   varieties of *B. semperflorens*, of which a few are · Atropur-
   purea (deep red), Diadem (dark rose), Illustration (carmine),
   Mme. Rene Cailleux, Lucianæ, etc.
ROEZLII —Dark scarlet; an old but fine kind.
SCHARFFIANA.—Large leaves and white flowers; distinct.
SEMPERFLORENS.—Very useful; dense green foliage; white
   flowers.
S. GIGANTEA CARMINEA.—An improved form of the foregoing,
   with much larger and very showy flowers of a carmine or rosy
   crimson hue.
S GIGANTEA ROSEA.—Similar, but of a soft rosy red.
S ROSEA.—Similar, but with rosy blossoms.
S. RUBRA.—Ditto, soft red
SUTHERLANDI.—Bright orange, distinct and pretty.
TRIOMPHE DE LEMOINE (Lawrence). — A variety with large
   flowers of a delicate rose colour, very freely produced.   A fit
   companion for Gloire de Sceaux.
UNDULATA (syn. *Comte H. de Limminge*).—Reddish-salmon,
   with prettily-marked foliage; habit drooping or trailing,
   rendering it a fine plant for baskets, as an edging for
   stages, etc.
WELTONIENSIS.—A pretty hybrid kind, raised by Col. Clarke
   many years ago; it has tuberous roots, and blossoms from
   May or June till Christmas, or later in a genial warmth.
   Pretty satiny foliage, red stems, and small pink blossoms; a
   fine kind for cut flowers.

   The varieties of *B. semperflorens* are now so numerous and
popular, and have attracted so much attention during the last
few years, as to demand a separate paragraph.   Their really
marvellous floriferousness—for they are truly perpetual
flowering—with their simplicity of culture, and adaptability for
many purposes, has rendered them universal favourites.   Most,
if not all, are easily raised, either from seed or cuttings, and
with good culture grow very rapidly, making beautiful little
specimens (especially from seed) in a short time, and frequently
commencing to flower in three or four months from the date of
sowing.
   In addition to their value as decorative plants for the greenhouse, conservatory, or window garden, most of the varieties are

also admirably adapted for bedding-out purposes, and if planted
out in any moderately rich and good soil, and a fairly warm
and sheltered situation, bloom profusely during the whole of the
summer, and until frost occurs, affording excellent effects of both
flowers and foliage, either alone or contrasted with the large-
flowered tuberous kinds; or with fine-foliaged plants of almost
any description. The charming variety known as "Vernon"
(*B. semp. atro-purpurea*) is exceptionally admirable in this
connection, forming a splendid bed or edging; this variety, as
well as the pink kind, is still flowering freely here in the open
air, at the middle of November. After the plants have done duty
in the flower garden during the summer, they may be lifted,
potted, and brought indoors, when they will continue flowering,
more or less, throughout the winter in any well-heated greenhouse or sunny window, though if the genial warmth of an
intermediate house or cool stove, with a temperature of 50 to
55deg at night can be afforded they will succeed decidedly
better at this season, and with a little care will form exceedingly
attractive objects.

The best in this class, beyond those already mentioned, are as
follows :—

AUREA (Bijou).—A pretty dwarf kind, with golden foliage.
BERTHA DE CHATEAU ROCHER.—A fine kind, with coral-
red flowers.
COMPACTA ALBA.—Very dwarf, with white flowers. *C nana*
has the same habit and red blossoms, and *C. aurea* has golden
foliage.
COURONNE LORRAINE.—Rosy carmine; very showy.
DIADEME.—Bright rose.
DR. CHASSAGNY (hybrid).
ELEGANS ALBA (Mdme. Martine).—White.
ELEGANTISSIMA.
ELEGANTISSIMA ALBA.
ENFANT DE LORRAINE —Rose.
ERFURTENKIND.—Pink.
GERBE FLEURI.—Brilliant red (hybrid).
GIGANTEA CARMINATA.—An exceedingly fine variety. First-
class Certificate and Award of Merit.
GLOIRE DE LORRAINE.—A hybrid variety, very floriferous and
showy.
ILLUSTRATION.—Carmine.
LA FRANCE.—Rose-colour.
LUCIANÆ.—Bright rose.
MULTIFLORA ALBA.—White.
MULTIFLORA FLORIBUNDA.—A rose-coloured hybrid; fine.
MULTIFLORA ROSEA.—Soft rose (hybrid).
NANA COMPACTA ROSEA.—Extra dwarf rose, only 3in. high.
SOUVENIR DE F. GOULON.—Coral-red.

TROPHIE.—Carmine-red.

VERNON (syn. *B. S. atro-purpurea*).—An exceedingly good variety of a very dwarf and compact habit, with numerous blossoms of a deep rosy-crimson hue, varying in depth with the season. The foliage also takes on a rich reddish-bronze or crimson hue when the plants are well exposed to air and sun in the summer. This makes a superb bedding plant. *Vernon compacta* is an extra dwarf form of this plant, and *Jules Brusson, Triomphe de Perreux*, and *Zulu King* are other fine forms.

DOUBLE-FLOWERING SEMPERFLORENS VARIETIES.

Yet another section. and one that promises to prove of considerable importance—that consisting of a set of double-flowering varieties of *B. semperflorens*—was introduced in 1898. They are practically all the result of the labours of M. Lemoine, the well-known French hybridist.

In foliage they bear a considerable resemblance to the ordinary *Semperflorens* varieties, though in one or two instances they are rather thicker, or more fleshy. The habit, however, is taller, the plants averaging 2ft. to 2½ft in height (when in bloom in 7in. or 8in. pots), and bearing freely pretty rosette-like blossoms about 1¼in. in diameter. Like the single kinds, they are practically perpetual-flowering, and blossoms as freely during the winter months (in a moderate warmth) as in the summer, in the greenhouse or out of doors.

The varieties are :

BIJOU DES JARDINS.—The first of this section sent out ; flowers of a deep red colour

BOULE DE NEIGE,—White blossoms, becoming tinged with pink in the open air ; leaves bright green.

GLOIRE DU MONTEL.—Deep rose. tinged with red ; flowers very double. Foliage green, becoming slightly tinged with bronze in the open air.

NANCY.—A beautiful, delicate rose-colour, very double. Leaves green ; habit fairly dwarf and very bushy.

TRIOMPHE DE LORRAINE.—Dark carmine-red, lighter under glass ; foliage bronzy, almost crimson outside.

Climbing Begonias.

Climbing Begonias.—To some the idea of climbing Begonias may appear absurd, but if the following varieties are planted out in a well-drained bed or border of light, rich soil, such as a mixture of good loam and leaf mould (or peat) in equal parts, with a little decayed manure and plenty of sand, they will soon begin to push up numerous strong sucker-like growths from the base, and if these are trained to wires or strings strained near the roof of the structure, they will run several feet, and produce numerous as well as extremely large and handsome trusses of variously-coloured blossoms.

Plenty of water must be given in hot summer weather, and during the winter also the soil should be kept moderately moist. Temperature should range about 55deg. at night (in the winter), with a rise of 5 to 10deg. or more during the day.

CAROLINEÆFOLIA.
CASTANEÆFOLIA.—Rose.
CORALLINA.—Vermilion ; makes a splendid climber.
DUKE OF YORK.—Reddish-pink.
GLAUCOPHYLLA.
PRES. CARNOT.—A variety of *Corallina*, with rich rosy-carmine blossoms in huge trusses; a grand climber.
PRINCE OF WALES.
PRINCESS OF WALES.
THE QUEEN.—Rosy-pink.

Bedding Begonias.

Bedding Begonias.—For bedding purposes Begonias are being employed in increasing numbers every year, and with satisfactory results. If possible one variety should be confined to a bed, because the effect at flowering time is vastly superior to that in which several sorts are planted in the same bed. As edgings to subjects of rather taller habit they are well suited, a form of culture that might be extended with benefit to the Flower Garden generally. Additional varieties are :—

ARGUS.—Flowers scarlet, thrown well above the foliage.
BAVARIA.—A free-growing variety of dwarf sturdy habit, with handsome foliage and pretty rosy-carmine flowers.
*BERTINI.—This reminds one of *B. Worthiana* It is of excellent habit, and bears warm orange-coloured flowers.
COUNT ZEPPLIN.—One of the finest of the section, and a gem for pot culture as well. It is dwarf, compact, and bears a profusion of medium-sized double scarlet flowers on stiff, erect stems, well above the metallic-coloured foliage. Flowers from early summer until autumn.
CRIMSON PET.—Though but a few inches high it produces an abundance of small crimson flowers over the rich foliage.
GLADIATEUR.—Flowers deep crimson, of excellent shape. Very free
HOLLYHOCK.—Flowers salmon-pink, borne throughout summer. A splendid variety.
PHOSPHORESCENS.—Of compact, branching habit and exceedingly floriferous. Its bright scarlet flowers are borne for several months together, and completely hide the foliage.
PINK PET.—Similar in habit to the preceding.
YELLOW PET.—Another variety of the same class as the two preceding.

CHAPTER XI.

THE REX VARIETIES.

THIS is a class of fibrous-rooted and evergreen plants, with large, heart-shaped oblique leaves that are deeply veined on the front or upper surface, and heavily nerved at the back, being also beautifully and variously marked above with blotches of silvery-white on a grey or dark green ground, and in other ways and shades also; while the under-surface is usually more or less stained with crimson and, as well as the leaf-stalks and stems, thickly furnished with stout hairs of the same colour. They are highly attractive and ornamental, and when seen in a good condition will bear comparison with any other fine-foliaged subjects to be found in our greenhouses and stoves. The flowers, which are chiefly produced during the late summer and autumn, though small and comparatively inconspicuous, as well as often hidden by the leaves, are really very beautiful, being of a pearly white or blush colour, and remarkably delicate and transparent in texture.

The whole of this really charming, though at present somewhat neglected, class of Begonias, owe the greater part of their parentage to the original species *B. rex* (itself a decidedly handsome plant—see Fig. 13, p. 79—and worth a place in any collection), this having been crossed with one or two other species in the first place, and hybrid seedlings being since raised again and again from the progeny. They are all of a more or less dwarf and compact habit, with short, thick stems, and when grown on and moved into large pots, instead of running up, they spread out into huge masses with many crowns, and often develop really enormous leaves. Those, however, who have no room for such large specimens will find quite small plants, even with three or four leaves only, quite as attractive as and often much better coloured than the large ones.

The proper place for these plants is in the intermediate house or cool stove, where they remain in beauty more or less all the year round. They may be grown well in any moderately warm greenhouse, and with proper treatment

FIG 13   BEGONIA REX.

can here be had in excellent condition during the summer and autumn; but as the winter draws on they lose their leaves, entirely or in part, when kept in a low temperature. In the strong heat of a stove, and especially with an atmosphere laden with moisture and heavy shade, though the growth is free and rapid, it is too diffuse, the leaves lose in both colour and substance, while if removed to a drier or more airy atmosphere the plants flag or wilt badly.

Shade from all strong sunshine must be given, certainly from March till October, as any over-exposure causes the leaves to lose their satiny brightness and to assume a dull and lustreless appearance, while under an extremely powerful sun they will scorch badly.   At the same time, if unduly deprived of light, they lack substance and colour also, so that it is important in securing well and richly-coloured foliage to hit the mean between the two extremes of too much light and sun and too little.   A moderately moist atmosphere is also necessary, for in an over-dry one the plants are liable to become infested with thrips, which quickly spoil their appearance ; but this again must not be overdone, or the tissue of the foliage will be rendered too soft.   Syringing the plants overhead, except perhaps to a slight extent while still young, or when just starting into fresh growth, is not to be recommended, and should be avoided if sufficient atmospheric moisture can be maintained by other means—*e.g.*, by damping the paths, floor, or stages, or by the use of tanks or pans of water placed in the house. Even perfectly clean rain-water is apt to leave the foliage spotted, and in any case overhead watering is detrimental to the richest colouring and to the delicate satiny " bloom " that is so much admired.

As regards soil, these Begonias are not at all particular, and will grow well in either loam or peat, plenty of sand being used in either case.   They make a decidedly freer growth in peat, but in loam the plants will be found more compact and substantial and the colours brighter.   On the whole, it is advisable to employ a mixed compost, such as equal parts of loam and peat, with half-a-part of leaf-mould and an equal quantity of sharp sand added.   To provide sufficient nourishment and ensure porosity, drain the pots well, and make the soil fairly firm.   When in full growth plenty of water must be given, and a little soot dissolved in it occasionally will keep the plants in health and ensure well-coloured foliage.

The plants may either be grown in pots or planted out, say, in the crevices of rock-work, where, with some nice light, sandy, peaty soil about their roots they thrive luxuriantly.   They associate well with ferns, especially where these are grown in a moderately warm temperature of 60deg. to 80deg., with light shade and a fair amount of atmospheric moisture. Another pretty way to grow these plants is in pockets (formed of wood, cork, or the patent wall-tiles) fixed against the back or end wall of a fernery or warm greenhouse, intermixed with ferns and other plants of a drooping nature.

Propagation may be effected by means of either shoot or leaf cuttings, the latter mode being the better plan where the plants are to be raised in quantity. Large and well-matured but still healthy and vigorous leaves may be cut across the principal ribs or nerves in ten or a dozen places, and pegged or weighted down with stones on to the surface of a well-drained pan nearly filled with a light and very sandy and porous compost. If peat is not at hand, a mixture of loam, leaf-mould, cocoanut-fibre, and sand, will answer just as well. If placed in a warm and close atmosphere, kept fairly but not too moist, and carefully shaded, roots will be formed at every cut, and a tiny leaf will follow; when a little advanced the plantlets should be separated and inserted singly into small pots, using a similar compost, and keeping them warm and close until established and growing freely. Another way is to cut the leaves into pieces of moderate size, each containing a length of one of the principal nerves, and insert them to the depth of 1in., the lower or thickest end of the rib downwards, of course, in pots or pans prepared as above. With similar treatment most of them will strike root and grow. Or small leaves, with 1in. of stalk, may be inserted singly in small pots, or several in a larger size, in much the same manner, with a similar result.

Seed is not at all difficult to obtain if the plants are treated much as advised for the tuberous-rooted kinds, but not exposing them quite so freely to sun and air, and the seedlings are easily raised. It is in this way, of course, that all the new varieties are obtained. These "Rex" varieties ally themselves very readily with several of the other species, and in this fact an interesting field for hybridisation is found.

A dozen of the finest new or specially distinct and handsome varieties in this, the ornamental-leaved section, are the following:

BERTHA MACGREGOR.—Leaves long, pointed, and deeply notched. Centre of each leaf very dark, with a very broad

F

band of pure silver, and a narrow margin of bronze;
growth free and strong.

DECORA.—A very dwarf variety, in the style of *B. rex*, but
with smaller leaves and stems. Leaves pointed, of a bronzy-
olive or metallic-brownish colour, strongly marked with
greenish-yellow along the mid-rib and principal nerves.

DR. JAMES.—Leaves of a satiny greyish-white ; dark metallic-
green margin and veins. The edges of the leaves are deeply
serrated or incised.

FLORA HILL.—Leaves small ; body-colour green, with veins of
the same colour, the whole irregularly splashed with white.
A very pretty kind.

FRANÇOIS BUCHNER.—Large heart-shaped leaves of a light
green, edged bronzy-red ; bold zone of pearly-white. An
exquisite variety.

MME. CHOLET.—Bronzy-green leaves with silver blotches ; very
striking.

MME. GEORGES BRUANT.—Deep metallic bronzy-green, with
purplish-red centre and white spots.

MME. PATRY.—Ground colour of leaves white, with rose
markings, and margined with purple and black ; extra fine.

MME. P. N. BINOT.—Dark centre, silver zone, and broad margin
of purplish-green with white spots.

MRS. A. G. SHEPHERD.—Fine broad leaves, centre and edge
bronzy-red, the body being of a beautifully-shaded green hue
with a silky lustre.

MRS. E. BONNER.—Leaves evenly serrated ; colour light silvery
green, with margin and ribs of bronzy-red ; fine, bold habit.

PERLE HUMFELD.—An extremely handsome variety ; leaves of
a velvety green in varying shades, with a zone of bold silver
spots. Each leaf is bordered with six or eight deep and
beautifully-regular teeth or notches.

The following are a dozen of the best among the older
kinds :—Comtesse Louise d'Erdody, Diademe, Distinction,
F. Schneider, Lesoudsi, Louise Closon (extra fine), Mme.
Almagny (very good and distinct), Mme. Lebocq (extra),
Merville, Mina, Pres. Bell, and Rubella.

BEGONIA DISCOLOR. REX VARIETIES

This comparatively new section has been produced by
crossing the old B. discolor with some of the varieties of
B. rex. They possess the free growth and noble foliage
of B. discolor, with the handsome leaf-markings of B. rex,
while they also flower towards the autumn with great freedom. They may be easily and successfully grown in pots
in any moderately warm plant-house, where they form very

handsome specimens, while if planted out in rich soil and a half-shaded position in the open-air in summer, they grow with great vigour, and afford a very striking appearance.

A few of the finest kinds are :—

A. CARRIÈRE.—Silvery leaves, with green veins.
ADONIS.—Rosy-carmine, F.C.C.
AFTERGLOW.—Blue.
ALBO-PICTA.—Spotted.
ALEGATIÈRE.—Dark green, edged and spotted with silver.
ARGENTEA GUTTATA.—Spotted foliage.
ARGYROSTIGMA ELEGANTISSIMA.
ARGYROSTIGMA GIGANTEA.
ARTHUR MALET.—Extra fine, handsome foliage, F.C.C.
A. TENNYSON.—Leaves violet and green, with white spots and silver zone.
BAUMANNI (syn. *odoratissima*).—Pretty rose-coloured blossoms, very fragrant; foliage dark green, hirsute.
B. CARMINEA.—Carmine.
BEAUTY.—Silver-white leaves with dark centre, and green border spotted with white.
B. HYBRIDA.
BICOLOR.—Light rosy-lilac.
BIJOU DE GAUD.—Rose.
BISMARCKII.
BLACK PRINCE.—Very dark green leaves, with a few white spots.
B. LILACINA.—Lilac-rose.
BOUQUET PARFAIT.
BRUANTI ELEGANS.
BRUANTI ROSEA.
BRUANTI FLORIBUNDA.
BURCKEI.—Light pink.
CARMINATA.—Orange, dwarf habit.
CAROLINEÆFOLIA.—A climbing species.
CASTANEÆFOLIA.—Rose, a good climber.
COMTESSE DE MONTESQUIEU.—Enormous leaves, white, shaded rose, and veined with dark bronze-green.
COMTESSE DE NERVELLÈE.—White.
CORALLINA (syn. *coccinea*).—Vermilion, a fine climbing kind.
CORBEILLE DE FEU.—Coral-red.
CRIMSON GEM.—Crimson.
DAVIESI.—Pink, drooping flowers (quite distinct from the following).
DAVISI (species).—Brilliant orange-scarlet, very dwarf and free.

DIRECTEUR CRÉPIN.—Silvery-white ground, shaded rose, and veined bronze.

DISCOLOR (syn. *Evansiana*).—A tuberous-rooted, deciduous species, with large and handsome foliage, soft green above, crimson-red beneath, and numerous blossoms of a delicate bluish-pink hue.

DIVERSIFOLIA (*Henrici Martiana*).—Carmine-rose, a good bedding kind, if started early ; also fine for winter flowering, producing rich rosy-carmine.

DREGII (syn. *B. caffra* and *B. reniformis*).—White.

DUCHESS OF YORK.—Bright red, a fine climbing variety.

DUKE OF CAMBRIDGE.—A climbing variety.

DUKE OF YORK.—Reddish-pink, climbing habit.

EARL OF ANNESLEY'S FAVOURITE.—Bright coral-red, a good climber.

EMERAUDE —Bright green leaves, dotted with silver.

ENSIGN.—Bright rose-pink.

EXCELSIOR.—Coral-red, a hybrid of *Baumanni and Veitchi*.

EXCELSIOR COMPACTA.

FOLIOSA (syn. *Microphylla*).—White, drooping.

FROEBELII (species).—Rich scarlet dwarf, fine.

FUCHSIOIDES (syn. *Miniata*).—Coral-red.

FULGENS —Large, bright red flowers, with deeper edges, sweetly scented.

GERANIOIDES.—White flowers.

GLAUCOPHYLLA.—A climbing kind.

GLOIRE DE JONG.—Salmon-pink.

GLOIRE DE SCEAUX.—See p. 72

GOLIATH.—Blush-white.

GOURY.—Fine bronze-green foliage and bright rose blossoms, extra.

HAAGEANA.—Salmon-red, very free, with fine foliage, splendid. (*B. scharffiana* is frequently sold under this name, but is quite distinct.)

HAAGEANA ERECTA.

HAAGEANA SULPHUREA.—Yellow.

HERACLEICOTYLE.—Pink and White.

HYBRIDA ABONDANCE —Rose.

HYBRIDA BRUANTI.—White.

HYBRIDA MULTIFLORA (*floribunda*).—Rose, of the *Fuchsioides* type.

HYBRIDA ROSEA MULTIFLORA.—Rose.

HYBRIDA WELLSIANA.—Soft Red.

JEANNE D'ARC (*syn.Lynchiana*).—Rosy-pink.

LA NEIGE —A fine white kind.

LEOPARD.—Large leaves of a soft green, with white dots

LOUIS VAN HOUTTE.

LUSTRE,—Clear green, with grey extra eye.

MACULATA—Green foliage, with white spots and pale pink blossoms.

MARTIANA GRANDIFLORA.

MARTIANA PULCHERRIMA.—Bronzy foliage and rosy carmine flowers, fine.

MARTIANA RACEMIFLORA. — Bright satiny-rose-coloured blossoms in large trusses; a large-flowered and very handsome kind.

M. DELLA POSTA —Silvery-grey, veined with dark bronze.

MME. JUDIC.—Fine dark bronzy foliage, with silver dots.

MME. LIONNET.—Pale flesh-colour.

MANICATA AUREA VARIEGATA (Maculata).—A finely variegated form of Manicata.

MARGARITACEA —A handsome species.

MARGARITÆ.—Soft rose.

MASTODONTE.—Delicate rose.

METALLICA.—An evergreen species, with glossy foliage and white flowers.

METALLICA FOLIIS VARIEGATA.—Very handsome.

MINIATA.—A tuberous kind, like Boliviensis.

MIRA.

MRS. HEAL.—Rosy-carmine.

MYRA.—Bright carmine-rose.

NATALENSIS —Rose, shaded yellow.

NŒMI MALET.—Bronze-crimson.

OCTOPETALA.—White; anemone-like flowers.

OCTOPETALA FLEUR D'ANTOINNE.—Rose.

OCTOPETALA LA LORRAINE.—Carmine.

OCTOPETALA LEMOINEI.—Autumn-flowering.

OCTOPETALA NOBLESSE.—Rose. large.

OCTOPETALA SEMI-PLENA.—Semi-double.

OCTOPETALA VILLE DE NANCY —Purple-crimson.

ODORATISSIMA.—White, fragrant.

PEARCEI (species).—Small yellow flowers, and beautifully marbled dark-green foliage.

PARVIFLORA.—White, very free.

PAUL BRUANT.—Delicate rose.

PICTA —Bright red; leaves spotted white.

PICTANENSIS.—Like Scharffiana, but finer.

POLYANTHA.—Soft rose.

PRES. CARNOT.—A variety of Corallina; a splendid climbing Begonia

PRINCE OF WALES.—A fine climbing variety.

PRINCESS BEATRICE.—White, fine.

PRINCESS OF WALES.—A fine climber.

PROF. FORSTER.—Silvery-white leaves, with dark bronze centre.

PURPLE PERFECTION.—Deep bronze-green, with silver, violet and purple edge.

RICINIFOLIA.—Handsome bronzy foliage.
ROBUSTA PERFECTA.
SANGUINEA.—Fine foliage.
SATURNE.—Dark foliage.
SCHMIDTI.—Fibrous-rooted.
SCHMIDTI HYBRIDA ALBA.—White.
SCHMIDTI HYBRIDA ROSEA (syn. *Versaillensis*).—Rose-colour.
SILVER QUEEN.—Blush-white.
SOCOTRANA (species).—Bright rose, distinct.
SUAVEOLENS.—Fragrant.
SUBPELTATA ALBA.—White.
SUBPELTATA VIOLESCENS.—Violet-rose.
THE QUEEN.—Pink, fine climbing variety.
VEITCHI.—Tuberous-rooted; fine cinnabar-red.
VERSCHAFFELTII.—Rose.
WELTONIENSIS.—Light pink flowers, and pretty satiny foliage;
    tuberous-rooted.
WORTHIANA.—Orange-scarlet, small flowers, but very free,
    makes a fine bed.
WORTHIANA (Hampton Court variety).—Extra fine.
WORTHIANA (White Underhill variety).—White, fine.

MISCELLANEOUS VARIETIES.

These are very numerous and varied in appearance and
character, some having tuberous, and others fibrous, roots,
while some are evergreen (more or less) and others deciduous.
Several are remarkable for beauty of foliage, whilst of others
the flowers are more or less attractive, and of others again both
leaves and flowers are ornamental. Warm greenhouse culture
will suit any of them as a rule; soil, as recommended for the
"Rex" section. Many of them make capital window plants.
Propagation in most cases is easily effected by means of
cuttings; in some instances bulbils are produced in the axils
of the leaves, and with ordinary care these seldom fail to grow
and make good plants. The old Beefsteak Begonia (*B. discolor*),
with large and nearly smooth leaves, green above, and of a
reddish-crimson below, is a good example of the latter class.
It has a tuberous root, and the annual stems are smooth,
dotted, and striped with red on a green ground. Towards
the autumn the small seed-like bulbils, of a deep brown
colour, are freely produced in the axils of the leaves, and
when the stems and leaves fall these should be gathered,
stored in sand or cocoanut-fibre for the winter, and placed
in well-drained pots of light sandy soil, in heat, to start in
the spring. Plants of this Begonia from tubers three or four
years old, and well grown, attain quite handsome proportions.
I have seen them quite 5ft. high, with stems as thick as a

broom-handle and leaves 18in. to 2ft. in length. The flowers, which are of a delicate rosy-pink and about 1in. across, are by no means unhandsome. This, with *B. metallica*, *B. weltoniensis*, and a few others, are among the best of window plants.

Those marked with a * have ornamental foliage, and those marked thus † are suitable for bedding-out purposes during the summer.

*ARTHUR MALET.—Extra fine.

†ASCOTENSIS.—An evergreen variety, with pink flowers; a grand bedder in a fine season.

†CONSTANTÆFOLIA.—Evergreen ; good bedder.

DISCOLOR.—Tuberous-rooted.

GERANIOIDES.—White flowers.

MACULATA.—Green foliage, with white spots and pale pink blossoms.

METALLICA.—An evergreen kind, with white flowers.

*METALLICA FOLIIS VARIEGATA.—Variegated foliage.

*NOEMI MALET.

*PICTA.—Pointed foliage with white spots.

*SANGUINEA.—Fine foliage.

SCHARFFIANA.—White flowers and large leaves.

SCHMIDTI.—Fibrous-rooted.

†WELTONIENSIS.—Tuberous-rooted, with pink flowers and pretty foliage ; makes a good bedder.

†WORTHIANA.—Small orange-scarlet flowers ; an old tuberous variety, of drooping habit, but makes a splendid bed.

B. semperflorens also makes a good bedder in light soil and a warm season. There is also a hybrid variety, the result of a cross between *B. semperflorens* and *B. Schmidti*, which was raised and sent out by Messrs. Sutton and Sons, of Reading, that is excellent for this purpose. It is called Princess Beatrice, and has pink flowers

[WINTER-FLOWERING VARIETIES.]

AGATHA (Socotrana ♀ ; Moonlight ♂).—Plant of sturdy habit, very free-flowering. Flowers deep pink, larger than those of the first-named parent. Leaves deep green, similar to those of *B. Socotrana*, but not peltate.

AGATHA COMPACTA (Socotrana × Natalensis).—Very compact and floriferous. Flowers similar to those of Gloire de Lorraine.

FRŒBELI INCOMPARABILIS.—Flowers rich scarlet, borne on erect stalks, 18in. to 2ft. long. Leaves large, obliquely heart-shaped.

IDEALA (Socotrana × Tuberous-rooted variety).—A splendid acquisition, with bold semi-double rosy-carmine flowers nearly 2in. across, borne on very stout stems well above the foliage.

JULIUS (Socotrana × Tuberous-rooted variety).—Large trusses of handsome salmon-rose double flowers, borne in great profusion.

WINTER CHEER (Socotrana × Scarlet Tuberous-rooted variety). Plant of strong growth, with deep green leaves and bright carmine flowers 3in. in diameter.

WINTER GEM (Socotrana × Scarlet Tuberous-rooted variety). —Dwarf and compact as to habit, with vivid-scarlet persistent flowers thrown well above the foliage.

WINTER PERFECTION (Socotrana × Tuberous-rooted variety). —Flowers large, semi-double, salmon-pink, suffused with rose. Of good habit and very free.

[GLOIRE DE LORRAINE VARIETIES.]

ALBA GRANDIFLORA.— Plant of strong growth; very free. Flowers large, white, tinted with pink, especially when first expanded, carried on strong stems well above the foliage.

MRS. LEOPOLD DE ROTHSCHILD.—Flowers pink; of compact, bushy habit and very free.

TURNFORD HALL.—A superb variety, with substantial white flowers, flushed with rose-pink, and passing to a paler shade near the margins of the petals.

[FOLIAGE BEGONIAS]

DIADEMA.—A species from Borneo, having deeply-cut glossy green leaves, blotched with white.

GLAUCOPHYLLA.—One of the best sorts for basket culture.

*PLATANIFOLIA DECORA.—A distinct variety, with deeply-lobed green leaves, heavily suffused with glaucous-grey.

PLATANIFOLIA ILLUSTRIS.—Pale green, deeply-lobed leaves, liberally streaked and spotted with grey. Stems brownish-red.

REX CONSPICUUM.—Dark olive-green leaves, heavily flushed with silver and mottled with grey; margins and veins blood-red.

REX MADAME A. PERNELLE.— Bronze-green leaves, freely spotted with white. Distinct and handsome.

REX MRS. F. SANDER.—A magnificent variety, with large leaves, crimson in the centre by footstalks, surrounded with rose-pink, and edged with bronze-green.

*REX MRS. JOHN LAING.—Leaves bronze-green, suffused with delicate pink, and bordered with pale green.

REX SANDER'S MASTERPIECE.— A dwarf variety, with rich brownish-crimson leaves, edged with green.

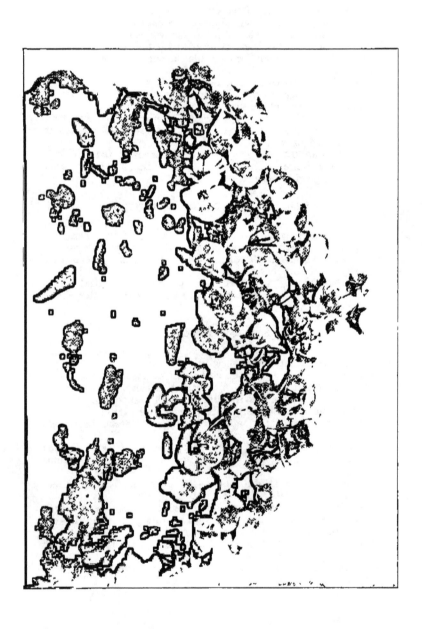

REX SOUVENIR DE JEAN BART. — Leaves large, the central portion light-grey, with a broad margin of bronze-green, freely spotted, and speckled with silvery-grey.

In conclusion, let me assure my readers that they will find the Begonia, in any of its numerous forms, and whether grown under glass or outside, a thoroughly satisfactory subject, that will amply repay whatever care and attention may be lavished upon it. It is a truly Protean plant, and any or all of the different species and varieties are fully as interesting, and in most cases as beautiful as they are varied. From a decorative point of view the tuberous-rooted hybrid forms undoubtedly bear away the palm, and no one who has not seen this class, as grown by Messrs. Blackmore & Langdon, at Twerton Hill Nursery, Bath; Mr. Cannell, at Swanley; Mr. T. S. Ware, of Feltham; or by the Messrs. Laing, at Forest Hill, can have any idea of what they are capable. At any of the places mentioned they may be seen during July, August, and September, growing in the open ground by the acre, and flowering profusely, as well as in thousands under glass, and a visit is certain to be found at once delightful and profitable by any true lover of floral beauty.

INDEX.

INDEX

To the Practical Handbooks
Published by L. Upcott Gill, London, and Chas. Scribner's Sons, New York.

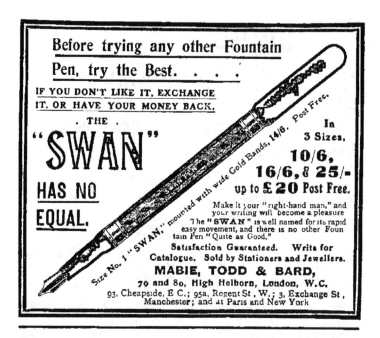
Public Opinion.

PUBLISHED EVERY FRIDAY.

Price 2d., by post 2½d.

REGISTERED FOR TRANSMISSION IN UNITED KINGDOM.

CONTENTS.

NEWS OF THE WEEK—AT HOME AND ABROAD.

NOTES ON POLITICAL EVENTS OF THE DAY.

LETTERS TO EMINENT MEN.

TOPICS OF THE WEEK,

Embracing subjects of keen interest to all men and women who would
learn more of the doings of the world at large, and the views of
the Leading Writers the world over on all questions of the day.

HENRY J. DRANE, Bell's Buildings, Fleet Street, London, E.C.

Catalogue of
Practical Handbooks

Published by

L. Upcott Gill, Bazaar Buildings, London, and
Chas. Scribner's Sons, New York.

American Daintles, and How to Prepare Them. By AN AMERICAN LADY
  In paper, price 1/-, by post 1/2.

Angler, Book of the All-Round. A Comprehensive Treatise on Angling in
  both Fresh and Salt Water. By JOHN BICKERDYKE With over 220 Engravings
  In cloth gilt, price 5/6, by post 5/10 Also in Four Divisions as follow —

Angling for Coarse Fish. Bottom Fishing, according to the Methods in
  use on the Thames, Trent, Norfolk Broads, and elsewhere. New Edition,
  Revised and Enlarged Illustrated In paper, price 1/-, by post 1/2.

Angling for Pike. The most approved methods of Fishing for Pike or Jack
  New Edition, Revised and Enlarged. Profusely illustrated. In paper,
  price 1/-, by post 1/2.

Angling for Game Fish. The Various Methods of Fishing for Salmon;
  Moorland, Chalk stream, and Thames Trout; Grayling and Char. New
  Edition Well illustrated. In paper, price 1/6, by post 1/9.

Angling in Salt Water. Sea Fishing with Rod and Line, from the Shore,
  Piers, Jetties, Rocks, and from Boats; together with Some Account of
  Hand-Lining. Over 50 Engravings. In paper, price 1/-, by post 1/2.

Angler, The Modern. A Practical Handbook on all Kinds of Angling, both
  Fresh Water and Sea By "OTTER." Well illustrated Third Edition
  In cloth gilt, price 2/6, by post 2/9.

Antiquities, English. A Popular Guide to the Collection of Curios of the
  Paleolithic, Neolithic, Bronze, Iron, Anglo-Saxon, and Mediæval Times, with
  a concise Dictionary of Terms, &c, used By GEORGE CLINCH, F G S., Author
  of "Old English Churches" Illustrated. In cloth, price 6/6, by post 6/10

Aquaria, Book of. A Practical Guide to the Construction, Arrangement, and
  Management of Freshwater and Marine Aquaria; containing Full Informa-
  tion as to the Plants, Weeds, Fish, Molluscs, Insects, &c, How and Where to
  Obtain Them, and How to Keep Them in Health By REV. GREGORY
  C BATEMAN, A K C, and REGINALD A. R. BENNETT, B.A. Illustrated. In cloth
  gilt, price 5/6, by post 5/10

Aquaria, Freshwater: Their Construction, Arrangement, Stocking, and
  Management Second Edition, revised and enlarged. By REV G C. BATE
  MAN, A K C Fully Illustrated. In cloth gilt, price 3/6, by post 3/10

Aquaria, Marine: Their Construction, Arrangement, and Management By
  R A R BENNETT, B A Fully Illustrated In cloth gilt, price 2/6, by
  post 2/9.

Autograph Collecting: A Practical Manual for Amateurs and Historical
  Students, containing ample information on the Selection and Arrangement
  of Autographs, the Detection of Forged Specimens, &c., &c., to which are
  added numerous Facsimiles for Study and Reference, and an extensive
  Valuation Table of Autographs worth Collecting. By HENRY T. SCOTT, M D,
  L R C P, &c. In cloth gilt, price 5/-, by post 5/4

Bazaars and Fancy Fairs: Their Organization and Management. A
  Secretary's Vade Mecum By JOHN MUIR. In paper, price 1/-, by post, 1/2.

All Books are Nett.

Bee-Keeping, Book of. A very practical and complete Manual on the Proper Management of Bees, especially written for Beginners and Amateurs who have but a few Hives By W. B WEBSTER, First class Expert, B B K A Fully illustrated. *In paper, price 1/-, by post 1/2, in cloth, price 1/6, by post 1/8.*

Bees and Bee-Keeping: Scientific and Practical By F R CHESHIRE, F L S, F R M S, Lecturer on Apiculture at South Kensington *In two vols., cloth gilt, price 16s , by post 16s. 6d.*

  Vol I., Scientific. A complete Treatise on the Anatomy and Physiology of the Hive Bee *In cloth gilt, price 7s 6d , by post 7s 10d*

  Vol. II., Practical Management of Bees. An Exhaustive Treatise on Advanced Bee Culture   [Out of Print

Begonia Culture, for Amateurs and Professionals. Containing Full Directions for the Successful Cultivation of the Begonia, under Glass and in the Open Air By B C RAVENSCROFT. New Edition, Revised and Enlarged With New Illustrations *In paper, price 1/-, by post 1/2*

Bent Iron Work: A Practical Manual of Instruction for Amateurs in the Art and Craft of Making and Ornamenting Light Articles in imitation of the beautiful Mediæval and Italian Wrought Iron Work By F J ERSKINE Illustrated *In paper, price 1/-, by post 1/2*

Birds, British, for the Cages and Aviaries. A Handbook relating to all British Birds which may be kept in Confinement. Illustrated By DR W. T GREENE *In cloth gilt, price 3/6, by post 3/10*

Birds' Eggs of the British Isles A comprehensive Guide to the Collector of British Birds' Eggs, with hints respecting the preparation of specimens for the cabinet Collated and compiled by ARTHUR G. BUTLER, Ph D , F L S., F Z S , F E S , from his larger work, "British Birds with their Nests and Eggs " Beautifully Illustrated with twenty-four full page plates in colour *In demy 4to, cloth gilt, price 10/6, by post 10/11.*

Birds, Favourite Foreign, for Cages and Aviaries How to Keep them in Health By W T GREENE, M A , M D , F Z S , &c Fully Illustrated *In cloth gilt, price 2/6, by post 2/9*

Boat Building and Sailing, Practical. Containing Full Instructions for Designing and Building Punts, Skiffs, Canoes, Sailing Boats, &c Particulars of the most suitable Sailing Boats and Yachts for Amateurs, and Instructions for their Proper Handling Fully Illustrated with Designs and Working Diagrams By ADRIAN NEISON, C E , DIXON KEMP A I N A and G CHRISTOPHER DAVIES *In one vol , cloth gilt, price 7/6, by post 7/10* Also in separate Vols as follows

Boat Building for Amateurs, Practical. Containing Full Instructions for Designing and Building Punts, Skiffs, Canoes, Sailing Boats, &c Fully Illustrated with Working Diagrams By ADRIAN NEISON, C E Second Edition, Revised and Enlarged by DIXON KEMP, Author of "A Manual of Yacht and Boat Sailing, '&c *In cloth gilt, price 2/6, by post 2/9.*

Boat Sailing for Amateurs, Practical. Containing Particulars of the most Suitable Sailing Boats and Yachts for Amateurs, and Instructions for their Proper Handling, &c. Illustrated with numerous Diagrams By G CHRISTOPHER DAVIES Second Edition, Revised and Enlarged, and with several New Plans of Yachts. *In cloth gilt, price 5/-, by post 5/4*

Bookbinding for Amateurs: Being descriptions of the various Tools and Appliances Required, and Minute Instructions for their Effective Use By W J E. CRANE Illustrated with 156 Engravings *In cloth gilt, price 2/6, by post 2/9*

Breeders' and Exhibitors' Record, for the Registration of Particulars concerning Pedigree Stock of every Description By W. K. TAUNTON In 3 Parts Part I , The Pedigree Record. Part II , The Stud Record. Part III , The Show Record *In cloth gilt, price each Part 2/6, or the set 6/ , by post 6 6*

Bridge, How to Win at. A Popular and Practical Guide to the Game. By "CUT-CAVENDISH.' Fourth Edition. *In stiff paper cover, price 1/-, by post 1/1*

Bridge: Its Whys and Wherefores. The Game taught by *Reason* instead of by Rule, on the same popular lines as "Scientific Whist" and "Solo Whist," and by the same Author, C J MELROSE With Illustrative Hands in Colours New and Revised Edition *In cloth gilt, price 3/6, by post 3/10 , in half leather, gilt top, price 5/6 by post 5/10.*

Bulb Culture, Popular. A Practical and Handy Guide to the Successful Cultivation of Bulbous Plants, both in the Open and Under Glass. By W D DRURY Second Edition Fully illustrated *In paper price 1/-. by post 1/2*

Bunkum Entertainments: A Collection of Original Laughable Skits on Conjuring, Physiognomy, Juggling, Performing Fleas, Waxworks, Panorama, Phrenology, Phonograph, Second Sight Lightning Calculators, Ventriloquism, Spiritualism, &c, to which are added Humorous Sketches, Whimsical Recitals, and Drawing-room Comedies By ROBERT GANTHONY Illustrated *In cloth, price 2/6, by post 2/9*

Butterflies, The Book of British: A Practical Manual for Collectors and Naturalists Splendidly illustrated throughout with very accurate Engravings of the Caterpillars, Chrysalids, and Butterflies, both upper and under sides, from drawings by the Author or direct from Nature By W J LUCAS, B A *In cloth gilt, price 2/6, by post 2/9.*

Butterfly and Moth Collecting: Being Practical Hints as to Outfit, most profitable Hunting Grounds, and Best Methods of Capture and Setting, with brief descriptions of many species Second Edition, revised, re-arranged, and enlarged Illustrated *In paper, price 1/, by post 1/2.*

Cabinet Making for Amateurs. Being clear Directions How to Construct many Useful Articles such as Brackets, Sideboard, Tables, Cupboards, and other Furniture Illustrated *In cloth gilt, price 2/6, by post 2/9*

Cactus Culture for Amateurs: Being Descriptions of the various Cactuses grown in this country, with Full and Practical Instructions for their Successful Cultivation By W WATSON, Assistant Curator of the Royal Botanic Gardens, Kew New Edition Profusely illustrated *In cloth gilt, price 5/-, by post 5/4*

Cage Birds, Diseases of: Their Causes, Symptoms, and Treatment. A Handbook for everyone who keeps a Bird By DR W T. GREENE, F Z S *In paper, price 1/-, by post 1/2*

Cage Birds, Notes on. Second Series Being Practical Hints on the Management of British and Foreign Cage Birds, Hybrids, and Canaries By various Fanciers. Edited by DR. W T. GREENE *In cloth gilt, price 6/-, by post 6/6.*

Canary Book. The Breeding, Rearing, and Management of all Varieties of Canaries and Canary Mules and all other matters connected with this Fancy By ROBERT L WALLACE Third Edition, with Coloured Frontispiece. *In cloth gilt, price 5/-, by post 5/4.*

Canaries, General Management of. Cages and Cage-making, Breeding, Managing, Mule Breeding, Diseases and their Treatment, Moulting, Pests, &c Illustrated. *In cloth gilt, price 2/6, by post 2/9*

Canaries, Exhibition. Full Particulars of all the different Varieties, their Points of Excellence, Preparing Birds for Exhibition, Formation and Management of Canary Societies and Exhibitions Illustrated. *In cloth gilt, price 2/6, by post 2/9.*

Canary-Keeping for Amateurs. A Book for the Average Canary-Keeper Plain and Practical Directions for the Successful Management and Breeding of Canaries as Pets rather than for Exhibition By DR W T GREENE, F Z S *In paper, price 1/, by post 1/2.*

Cane Basket Work: A Practical Manual on Weaving Useful and Fancy Baskets By ANNIE FIRTH Series I and II Illustrated *In cloth gilt, price 1/6, by post 1/8 each*

Card Tricks. By HOWARD THIRSTON A Manual on the Art of Conjuring with Cards, including many hitherto unpublished Novel and Unique Experiments, as presented by the Author in the Leading Theatres of the World. Illustrated *In paper, price 2/6, by post 2/8, in cloth, price 3 5 by post 3/9*

Card Tricks, Book of, for Drawing-room and Stage Entertainments by Amateurs, with an exposure of Tricks as practised by Card Sharpers and Swindlers. Numerous Illustrations By PROF. R KUNARD. *In stiff boards, price 2/6, by post 2/9*

Carnation Culture, for Amateurs The Culture of Carnations and Picotees of all Classes in the Open Ground and in Pots By B C. RAVENSCROFT Third Edition. Illustrated. *In paper, price 1/-, by post 1/2*

Cats, Domestic and Fancy. A Practical Treatise on their Varieties, Breeding, Management, and Diseases By JOHN JENNINGS Second Edition, Revised and Enlarged Illustrated *In paper, price 1/-, by post 1/2.*

All Books are Nett

Chip-Carving as a Recreation A Practical Manual for Amateurs, containing a Full and Clear Description of the Manipulation and Use of the Tools, with a Chapter on the Principles and Construction of Designs By W JACKSON SMITH Profusely Illustrated with Specially Prepared Illustrations, showing how the Tools should be Held and Used, and the way to Prepare Designs. *In paper, price 1/-, by post 1/2.*

Chrysanthemum Culture, for Amateurs and Professionals Containing Full Directions for the Successful Cultivation of the Chrysanthemum for Exhibition and the Market. By B. C RAVENSCROFT Third Edition. Illustrated *In paper, price 1/-, by post 1/2*

Chrysanthemum, The Show, and Its Cultivation. By C. SCOTT, of the Sheffield Chrysanthemum Society. *In paper, price 6d , by post 7d*

Churches, Old English: Their Architecture, Furniture, Decorations, Monuments, Vestments, and Plate, &c. Second and Enlarged Edition By GEO CLINCH, F.G.S. Magnificently illustrated. *In cloth gilt, price 6/6, by post 6/10*

Church Festival Decorations. Being full directions for Garnishing Churches for Christmas, Easter, Whitsuntide and Harvest, and notes on other Feasts and Festivals of the Church. Second Edition. Re-written and enlarged by ERNEST R SUFFLING Profusely illustrated. *In cloth, price 2/6, by post 2/9*

Chucks and Chucking. Being an Account of Chucks New and Old, and of How to Use Them, with a Description of Various Methods of Mounting Work in the Lathe. By H. J. S. CASSAL. Profusely Illustrated. *In paper, price 1/-, by post 1/2.*

Coffee Stall Management. Practical Hints for the Use of those Interested in Temperance or Philanthropic Work. *In paper, price 1/-, by post 1/1.*

Coins, a Guide to English Pattern, in Gold, Silver, Copper, and Pewter, from Edward I to Victoria, with their Value. By the REV. G. F CROWTHER, M A Illustrated *In silver cloth, with gilt facsimiles of Coins, price 5/-, by post 5/3*

Coins of Great Britain and Ireland, a Guide to the, in Gold, Silver, and Copper, from the Earliest Period to the Present Time, with their Value. By the late COLONEL W. STEWART THORBURN. Fourth Edition. Revised and Enlarged by H. A GRUEBER, F S A With 42 Plates, illustrating over 360 Coins. *In cloth gilt, price 10/6, by post 10/10.*

Cold Meat Cookery. A Handy Guide to making really tasty and much appreciated Dishes from Cold Meat. By MRS J E DAVIDSON. *In paper, price 1/-, by post 1/2*

Collie, The. As a Show Dog, Companion, and Worker By HUGH DALZIEL Revised by J. MAXTEE, Author of "Popular Dog Keeping," &c , &c Third Edition. Illustrated *In paper, price 1/-, by post 1/2*

Collie Stud Book. Edited by HUGH DALZIEL. *In cloth gilt, price 3/6 each, by post 3/9 each*
    Vol. I., containing Pedigrees of 1308 of the best-known Dogs, traced to their most remote known ancestors , Show Record to Feb , 1890, &c
    Vol. II. Pedigrees of 795 Dogs, Show Record, &c.
    Vol. III. Pedigrees of 786 Dogs, Show Record, &c

Conjuring, Book of Modern. A Practical Guide to Drawing-room and Stage Magic for Amateurs. By PROFESSOR R KUNARD Illustrated *In stiff boards, price 2/6, by post 2/9.*

Conjuring and Card Tricks, Book of. By PROF. R KUNARD Being "The Book of Modern Conjuring" and "The Book of Card Tricks" bound in one vol. *Cloth gilt, price 5/-, by post 5/4*

Conjuring for Amateurs A Practical Handbook on How to Perform a Number of Amusing Tricks, with diagrams, where necessary, to explain exactly how the trick is carried out By PROF ELLIS STANYON *In paper, price 1/- by post 1/2.*

Conjuring with Cards: Being Tricks with Cards, and How to Perform Them By PROF. ELLIS STANYON. Illustrated *In paper, price 1/-, by post 1/2.*

Cookery, The Encyclopædia of Practical. A complete Dictionary of all pertaining to the Art of Cookery and Table Service. Edited by THEO. FRANCIS GARRETT, assisted by eminent Chefs de Cuisine and Confectioners. Profusely Illustrated with Coloured Plates and Engravings by HAROLD FURNISS, GEO CRUIKSHANK, W MUNN ANDREW, and others *In demy 4to, half morocco, cushion edges,* 2 vols., price £3 3/-, carriage paid £3/4/6 , 4 vols., £3/13/6, carriage paid £3 15/-.

Cork-Grip Exercises, The Jappy System of. Without Dumb-bells or Developers With 24 Illustrations *In paper, price 6d , by post 7d*
(Cork Grips may be obtained through any Bookseller, or direct from the Publisher at 1/11 per pair)

Cucumber Culture for Amateurs. Including also clear Directions for the Successful Culture of Melons, Vegetable Marrows and Gourds By W. J. MAY New Edition, Revised and Enlarged, with new Illustrations. *In paper, price 1/-, by post 1/2.*

Cyclist's Route Map of England and Wales. Shows clearly all the Main, and most of the Cross, Roads, Railroads, and the Distances between the Chief Towns, as well as the Mileage from London. In addition to this, Routes of *Thirty of the Most Interesting Tours* are printed in red. Fourth Edition, thoroughly revised The map is printed on specially prepared vellum paper, and is the fullest, handiest, and best up-to-date tourist's map in the market. *In cloth, price 1/-, by post 1/2*

Dainties, English and Foreign, and How to Prepare Them. By MRS. DAVIDSON. *In paper, price 1/-, by post 1/2*

Dairy-Farming, Modern. A practical Handbook on the Management of the Milch Cow and the profitable Utilisation of Milk, for Students, Tenant Farmers, and Amateurs By H L PUXLEY Illustrated. *In cloth, price 3/6, by post 3/10.*

Designing, Harmonic and Keyboard. Explaining a System whereby an endless Variety of Most Beautiful Designs suited to numberless Manufactures may be obtained by Unskilled Persons from any Printed Music. Illustrated by Numerous Explanatory Diagrams and Illustrative Examples. By C. H WILKINSON. Cheap Edition. *In demy 4to, cloth gilt, price 10/-, by post 10/8.*

Dogs, Breaking and Training: Being Concise Directions for the proper education of Dogs, both for the Field and for Companions Second Edition By "PATHFINDER." With Chapters by HUGH DALZIEL. Many new Illustrations *In cloth gilt, price 6/6, by post 6/10*

Dogs, British. Their Points, Selection, and Show Preparation Third Edition. By W. D. DRURY, Kennel Editor of "The Bazaar," assisted by eminent specialists Beautifully Illustrated with full-page and other engravings of typical dogs of the present time, mostly produced from photographs of living dogs, and numerous smaller illustrations in the text This is the fullest work on the various breeds of dogs kept in England. In one volume, *demy 8vo, cloth gilt, price 12/6, by post 13/-.*

Dogs, Diseases of: Their Causes, Symptoms, and Treatment : Modes of Administering Medicines, Treatment in cases of Poisoning, &c For the use of Amateurs By HUGH DALZIEL. Fourth Edition. Entirely Re-written and brought up to date. *In paper, price 1/-, by post 1/2 , in cloth gilt, price 2/-, by post 2/3.*

Dog-Keeping, Popular: Being a Handy Guide to the General Management and Training of all Kinds of Dogs for Companions and Pets A New and Revised Edition. By J. MAXTEE Illustrated *In paper, price 1/-, by post 1/2.*

Dragonflies, British. Being an Exhaustive Treatise on our Native Odonata, Their Collection, Classification, and Preservation By W. J. LUCAS, B.A. Very fully Illustrated with 27 Plates, Illustrating 39 Species, exquisitely printed in Colour, and numerous Black-and-White Engravings. *In cloth gilt, price 31/6, by post 31/11.*

Egg and Poultry Raising. *See* "Poultry and Egg Raising," page 12.

Egg Dainties. How to Cook Eggs One Hundred and Fifty Different Ways, English and Foreign. *In paper, price 1/-, by post 1/2.*

Eggs Certificate, Fertility of. These are Forms of Guarantee given by the Sellers to the Buyers of Eggs for Hatching, undertaking to refund value of any unfertile eggs, or to replace them with good ones Very valuable to sellers of eggs, as they induce purchases *In books, with counterfoils, price 6d., by post 7d.*

Engravings and their Value. Containing a Dictionary of all the Greatest Engravers and their Works By J H SLATER Third Edition. Revised with an appendix and illustrations, and with latest Prices at Auction, &c *In cloth gilt, price 15/-, by post 15/5*

Entertainments, Amateur, for Charitable and other Objects: How to Organise and Work them with Profit and Success. By ROBERT GANTHONY. *In paper, price 1/-, by post 1/2.*

All Books are Nett

8   *Published by* L Upcott Gill, *London, and*

Feathered Friends, Old and New. Being the Experience of many years Observations of the Habits of British and Foreign Cage Birds By Dr. W. T. Greene Illustrated *In cloth gilt, price 5/-, by post 5/4*

Ferns, Choice, for Amateurs: Their Culture and Management in the Open and Under Glass Abridged from "The Book of Choice Ferns." By Geo. Schneider. With numerous Illustrations. *In cloth, price 3/6, by post 3 9*

Ferns, The Book of Choice: for the Garden, Conservatory, and Stove Describing the best and most striking Ferns and Selaginellæ, and giving explicit directions for their Cultivation, the formation of Rockeries, the arrangement of Ferneries, &c By George Schneider With 87 Coloured and other Plates and 396 Engravings of considerable artistic beauty *In 3 vols , large post 4to, cloth gilt, price £3 3/-, carriage paid £3 5/-.*

Ferrets and Ferreting. Containing Instructions for the Breeding, Managing, Training, and Working of Ferrets Fourth Edition. Revised and Enlarged Illustrated. *In paper, price 1/-, by post 1/2*

Finches, Beautiful Foreign, and Their Treatment in Captivity. By A G Butler, Ph.D. Edited by A H Mathew. Illustrated from Life by F. W Frohawk, with 60 full page plates, beautifully reproduced in colour *In Imp 8vo, cloth gilt, price 25/-, by post 25/6.*

Firework Making for Amateurs. A complete, accurate, and easily understood work on making Simple and High-class Fireworks By Dr. W H Browne, M A. *In coloured wrapper, price 2/6, by post 2/9.*

Fish, Flesh, and Fowl. When in Season, How to Select, Cook, and Serve. By Mary Barrett Brown. *In paper, price 1/ , by post 1/3*

Forge Work, Simple, for Amateurs and Others : A Practical Handbook for Beginners in the Blacksmith's Art By H J S Cassal Illustrated. *In paper, price 1/-, by post 1/2*

Fortune Telling by Cards. Describing and Illustrating the Methods by which the would-be occult Tells Fortunes by Cards. By J. B. Prangley Illustrated *In paper, price 1/-, by post 1/2*

Fox Terrier, The. Its History, Points, Breeding, Rearing, Preparing for Exhibition, and Coursing By Hugh Dalziel Second Edition, Revised and brought up to date by J. Maxtee (Author of " Popular Dog Keeping ") Fully illustrated. *In paper, price 1/-, by post 1/2 in cloth, with Coloured Frontispiece and several extra plates, price 2/6, by post 2 9*

Fox Terrier Stud Book. Edited by Hugh Dalziel. *In cloth gilt, price 3/6 each, by post 3/9 each*

     Vol. I., containing Pedigrees of over 1400 of the best-known Dogs, traced to their most remote known ancestors.

     Vol. II. Pedigrees of 1544 Dogs, Show Record, &c

     Vol. III. Pedigrees of 1214 Dogs, Show Record, &c.

     Vol. IV. Pedigrees of 1168 Dogs, Show Record, &c.

     Vol. V. Pedigrees of 1562 Dogs, Show Record, &c

Fretwork and Marquetry. A Practical Manual of Instructions in the Art of Fret-cutting and Marquetry Work By D. Denning Profusely Illustrated *In cloth gilt, price 2/6, by post 2/9*

Friesland Meres, A Cruise on the. By Ernest R. Suffling Illustrated *In paper, price 1/-, by post 1,2*

Fruit Culture for Amateurs. An illustrated practical hand-book on the Growing of Fruits in the Open and under Glass. By S T Wright With Chapters on Insect and other Fruit Pests by W D Drury Second Edition. Illustrated. *In cloth gilt price 3/6, by post 3/10*

Game Preserving, Practical. Containing the fullest Directions for Rearing and Preserving both Winged and Ground Game, and Destroying Vermin , with other information of Value to the Game Preserver. By W. Carnegie Illustrated, by F W Frohawk, M. I Lydon and others. *In cloth gilt, price 7/6, by post 7/11.*

Gardening, Dictionary of. A Practical Encyclopædia of Horticulture, for Amateurs and Professionals Illustrated with 3150 Engravings Edited by G Nicholson, Curator of the Royal Botanic Gardens, Kew ; assisted by Prof Trail, M D , Rev P W Myles, B A , F L S , W Watson, J. Garrett, and other Specialists *In 5 vols large print 4to Cloth gilt, price £4, carriage paid £4/1/6.*

Gardening, Home. A Manual for the Amateur, Containing Instructions for the Laying Out, Stocking, Cultivation, and Management of Small Gardens— Flower, Fruit, and Vegetable By W D DRURY, F R H S Illustrated *In paper, price 1/-, by post* 1/2

Gardening, Open-Air: The Culture of Hardy Flowers, Fruit, and Vegetables. Edited by W D DRURY, F E S Beautifully Illustrated *In demy 8vo, cloth gilt, price 6/-, by post 6/5.*

Gardening, the Book of: A Handbook of Horticulture By well-known Specialists, including J. M. Abbott, W G Baker, Charles Bennett, H J Chapman, James Douglas, Charles Friedrich, A Griessen, F. M. Mark, Trevor Monmouth, G Schneider, Mortimer Thorn, J. J Willis, and Alan Wynne Edited by W D DRURY (Author of "Home Gardening," "Insects Injurious to Fruit," "Popular Bulb Culture," &c.). Very fully Illustrated. 1 *vol , demy 8vo, cloth gilt, about* 1200*pp, price* 16/-, *by post* 16/8

Glues and Cements. A Practical Book on Making and Using Glues, Cements, and Fillings Invaluable in every Workshop By H J S. CASSAL (Author of "Chucks and Chucking," &c). Illustrated *In paper, price 1/ , by post* 1/2

Goat-Keeping for Amateurs: Being the Practical Management of Goats for Milking Purposes Abridged from "The Book of the Goat." Illustrated *In paper, price 1/-, by post* 1/2

Grape Growing for Amateurs. A Thoroughly Practical Book on Successful Vine Culture By E. MOLYNEUX. Illustrated. *In paper, price 1/-, by post* 1/2.

Greenhouse Construction and Heating. Containing Full Descriptions of the Various Kinds of Greenhouses, Stove Houses, Forcing Houses, Pits and Frames, with Directions for their Construction, and also Descriptions of the Different types of Boilers, Pipes, and Heating Apparatus generally, with Instructions for Fixing the Same. By B C RAVENSCROFT Illustrated *In cloth gilt, price* 3/6, *by post* 3/9

Greenhouse Management for Amateurs. The Best Greenhouses and Frames, and How to Build and Heat them, Illustrated Descriptions of the most suitable Plants, with general and Special Cultural Directions, and all necessary information for the Guidance of the Amateur. By W. J. MAY. Third Edition, Revised and Enlarged. Magnificently illustrated *In cloth gilt, price* 5/-, *by post* 5/4

Greyhound, The: Its History, Points Breeding, Rearing, Training, and Running By HUGH DALZIEL New Edition, edited by J MAXTEE, with special information on Training and Running by a well known courser *In paper, price 1/-, by post* 1/2

Guinea Pig, The, for Food, Fur, and Fancy Its Varieties and its Management By CUMBERLAND, F Z S Illustrated *In paper, price 1/ , by post* 1/2. *In cloth gilt, with coloured frontispiece, price* 2/6, *by post* 2/9

Handwriting, Character Indicated by. With Illustrations in Support of the Theories advanced, taken from Autograph Letters, of Statesmen, Lawyers, Soldiers, Ecclesiastics, Authors, Poets, Musicians, Actors, and other persons Second Edition By R BAUGHAN. *In cloth gilt, price* 2/6, *by post* 2/9

Hardy Perennials and Old-fashioned Garden Flowers. Descriptions, alphabetically arranged, of the most desirable Plants for Borders, Rockeries, and Shrubberies, including Foliage, as well as Flowering Plants. By J. WOOD Profusely Illustrated *In cloth gilt, price* 3/6, *by post* 3/10.

Hawk Moths, Book of British. A Popular and Practical Manual for all Lepidopterists Copiously illustrated in black and white from the Author's own exquisite Drawings from Nature By W J LUCAS, B A *In cloth gilt, price* 3/6, *by post* 3/9

Horse Buying and Management. A Practical Handbook for the Guidance of Amateurs in Buying a Horse, with Instructions as to its after management By HENRY E FAWCUS. Illustrated *In paper, price 1/, by post* 1/2.

Horse-Keeper, The Practical. By GEORGE FLEMING, C B LL D , F R C V S, late Principal Veterinary Surgeon to the British Army, and Ex-President of the Royal College of Veterinary Surgeons *In cloth gilt, price* 3/6, *by post* 3/10

Horse-Keeping for Amateurs A Practical Manual on the Management of Horses, for the guidance of those who keep one or two for their personal use. By FOX RUSSELL *In paper , price 1/-, by post* 1/2, *cloth gilt, price* 2/-, *by post* 2/3.

All Books are Nett.

Horses, Diseases of : Their Causes, Symptoms, and Treatment For the use of Amateurs. By HUGH DALZIEL. *In paper, price* 1/-, *by post* 1/2 ; *cloth gilt, price* 2/-, *by post* 2/2.

Incubators and their Management. By J H SUTCLIFFE Fifth Edition, Revised. Illustrated. *In paper, price* 1/-, *by post* 1/2.

Jack All Alone. Being a Collection of Descriptive Yachting Reminiscences. By FRANK COWPER, B A , Author of "Sailing Tours." Illustrated *In cloth gilt, price* 3/6, *by post* 3/10.

Jiu-Jitsu and other Methods of Self-Defence. Describing and Illustrating the Japanese Art of Jiu-Jitsu, with a section specially adapted to Ladies, together with a description of a number of Tricks of Self-Defence, well within the capacity of anyone. By PERCY LONGHURST, Author of "Wrestling in the Catch-Hold and Græco-Roman Styles " Profusely Illustrated. *In paper, price* 1/-, *by post* 1/2

Journalism, Practical. How to Enter Thereon and Succeed. A Book for all who think of "Writing for the Press " By JOHN DAWSON. A New and Revised Cheap Edition. *In paper, price* 1/-, *by post* 1/2.

Kennel Management, Practical. A Complete Treatise on the Proper Management of Dogs for the Show Bench, the Field, or as Companions, with a chapter on Diseases—their Causes and Treatment By W. D DRURY, assisted by well-known Specialists Illustrated *In cloth, price* 10/6, *by post* 11/-.

Lace, A History of Hand-Made. By MRS. F. NEVILL JACKSON. With Supplementary Remarks by SIGNOR ERNESTO JESURUM. Exquisitely Illustrated with over 200 high-class Engravings of Old and Valuable Laces and their application to Dress as shown in numerous Portraits and Monochrome and Sepia Plates of great beauty. *In crown* 4to, *cloth gilt, price* 18/-, *by post* 18/6 *Edition de Luxe, on large paper, containing* 12 *specimens of Real Lace, handsomely bound in full leather, gilt, price* £4 4/-, *by post* £4 5/-. (A few copies only left at this price, after which there are 60 at £5 5/-, when the entire stock will be exhausted)

Lawn Tennis, Secrets of : A useful Guide to the Training and Playing of Lawn Tennis, with special chapters on Diet, by F. W. PAYN *In cloth, price* 2/5, *by post* 2/10

Laying Hens, How to Keep, and to Rear Chickens in Large or Small Numbers, in Absolute Confinement, with perfect Success. By MAJOR G F. MORANT *In paper, price* 6d , *by post* 7d

Library Manual, The. A Guide to the Formation of a Library, and the Values of Rare and Standard Books By J H SLATER, Barrister-at-Law Third Edition Revised and Greatly Enlarged *In cloth gilt, price* 7/6, *by post* 7/10.

Magic Lanterns, Modern. A Guide to the Management of the Optical Lantern, for the Use of Entertainers, Lecturers, Photographers, Teachers, and others. By R CHILD BAYLEY *In paper, price* 1/-, *by post* 1/2.

Marqueterie Wood-Staining for Amateurs. A Practical Handbook to Marqueterie Wood-staining, and kindred Arts. By ELIZA TURCK Profusely Illustrated *In paper, price* 1/-, *by post* 1/2.

Medicine and Surgery, Home. A Dictionary of Diseases and Accidents, and their Proper Home Treatment. For Family Use. By W. J. MACKENZIE, M D. Illustrated. *In paper, price* 1/-, *by post* 1/2.

Mice, Fancy : Their Varieties, Management, and Breeding. Third Edition, with additional matter and Illustrations *In coloured wrapper representing different varieties, price* 1/-, *by post* 1/2

Model Yachts and Boats : Their Designing, Making, and Sailing. Illustrated with 118 Designs and Working Diagrams By J DU V. GROSVENOR. Cheap Edition. *In cloth gilt, price* 2/6, *by post* 2/9

Monkeys, Pet, and How to Manage Them. By ARTHUR PATTERSON. Illustrated. Cheap Edition, Revised. *In paper, price* 1/-, *by post* 1/2.

Mountaineering, Welsh. A Complete and Handy Guide to all the Best Roads and Bye-Paths by which the Tourist should Ascend the Welsh Mountains. By A W. PERRY. With Numerous Maps *In cloth gilt, price* 2/6, *by post* 2/9

Mushroom Culture for Amateurs. With Full Directions for Successful Growth in Houses, Sheds, Cellars, and Pots, on Shelves, and Out of Doors, including Pasture Lands By W. J. MAY. New Edition, thoroughly revised and with New Illustrations. *In paper, price* 1/-, *by post* 1/2.

Naturalists' Directory, The. Invaluable to all Students and Collectors. *In paper, price 1/6, by post 1/9. In cloth 2/-, by post 2/3*

Needlework, Dictionary of. An Encyclopædia of Artistic, Plain, and Fancy Needlework By S F A CAULFEILD and B. C SAWARD. Magnificently Illustrated with 41 Embossed and Coloured Plates of Lace, Raised, and other Needlework, besides a large number of Wood Engravings 528pp A cheap re-issue. *In demy 4to, with satin brocade, price 21/-, postage 10d. extra.*

Orchids: Their Culture and Management By W. WATSON (Curator, Royal Botanic Gardens, Kew) New Edition, thoroughly Revised and Enlarged. Contains Full Descriptions of all Species and Varieties that are in General Cultivation, a List of Hybrids and their Recorded Parentage, and Detailed Cultural Directions. By HENRY J. CHAPMAN, one of the finest growers and judges in the kingdom (member of the Orchid and Scientific Committees of the Royal Horticultural Society) Beautifully Illustrated with 180 Engravings and 20 Coloured Plates *In demy 8vo, cloth gilt extra, price 25/-, by post 25/6*

Painting, Decorative. A practical Handbook on Painting and Etching upon Textiles, Pottery, Porcelain, Paper, Vellum, Leather, Glass, Wood, Stone, Metals, and Plaster, for the Decoration of our Homes By B. C. SAWARD. *In cloth gilt, price 3/6, by post 3/10.*

Palmistry, Life Studies in. The hands of Notable Persons read according to the practice of Modern Palmistry By I OXENFORD Illustrated with 41 Full-Page Plates *In crown 4to, cloth gilt, price 5/-, by post 5/4*

Palmistry, Modern. By I OXENFORD, Author of Life Studies in Palmistry. Numerous Original Illustrations by L. WILKINS. Cheap Edition *In paper, price 1/-, by post 1/2.* [in the press

Paper Work, Instructive and Ornamental. A practical book on the making of flowers and many other articles for artistic decoration, including a graduated course of Paper Folding and Cutting for children five to twelve years of age. Especially useful as preparatory exercises to the making of artificial flowers in silk and velvet, increasing that dexterity of hand and niceness of finish so necessary to that work By MRS L WALKER. Fully Illustrated *In crown 4to, cloth gilt, price 3/6, by post 3/11*

Parcel Post Dispatch Book (registered). An invaluable book for all who send parcels by post Provides 99 Address Labels, Certificates of Posting, and Records of Parcels Dispatched. By the use of this book parcels are insured against loss or damage to the extent of £2. Authorised by the Post Office. *Price 1/-, by post 1/2, larger sizes if required.*

Parrakeets, Popular. How to Keep and Breed Them By W T GREENE, M.D, M A., F Z S, &c. *In paper, price 1/-, by post 1/2.*

Parrot, The Grey, and How to Treat it By W T GREENE, M.D., M A, F Z S., &c. *In paper, price 1/-, by post 1/2*

Patience, Games of, for one or more Players. How to Play 173 different Games of Patience. By M. WHITMORE JONES. Illustrated Series I, 39 games; Series II, 34 games; Series III, 33 games; Series IV., 37 games, Series V., 30 games. *Each, in paper, 1/-, by post 1/2. The five bound together, in cloth gilt, price 6/-, by post 6/4. In full leather, solid gilt edges, price 10/6, by post 10/11*

Pedigree Record, The. Being Part I of "The Breeders' and Exhibitors' Record," for the Registration of Particulars concerning Pedigrees of Stock of every Description By W. K TAUNTON *In cloth gilt, price 2/6, by post 2/9*

Photo Printing. A Practical Guide to Popular Photographic Printing Papers and their Treatment, dealing with the leading Kinds of P O P, Bromide, Platinotype, Carbon, Self-Toning, and Gas-light Papers By HECTOR MACLEAN, F.R P.S. Illustrated. *In paper, price 1/-, by post 1/2.*

Photography, Modern, for Amateurs. By J. EATON FEARN. A Practical Handbook for all Photographers except those advanced in the Art. Fifth Edition Revised and Enlarged by J MACINTOSH, Secretary to The Royal Photographic Society *In paper, price 1/-, by post 1/2.*

Pianos, Tuning and Repairing. The Amateur's Guide to the Practical Management of a Cottage or Grand Piano without the intervention of a Professional Third Edition, Revised and Enlarged *In paper, price 1/-, by post 1/2.*

Picture-Frame Making for Amateurs. Being Practical Instructions in the Making of various kinds of Frames for Paintings, Drawings, Photographs, and Engravings. By the REV. J. LUKIN. Illustrated. *In paper, price 1/-, by post 1/2*

All Books are Nett.

Pig, Book of the. The Selection, Breeding, Feeding, and Management of the Pig, the Treatment of its Diseases, The Curing and Preserving of Hams, Bacon, and other Pork Foods, and other information appertaining to Pork Farming. By Professor James Long. Fully Illustrated with Portraits of Prize Pigs, Plans of Model Piggeries, &c. New and Revised Edition. *In cloth gilt, price 6/5, by post 6/10.*

Pig-Keeping, Practical: A Manual for Amateurs based on personal Experience in Breeding, Feeding and Fattening, also in Buying and Selling Pigs at Market Prices. By R. D. Garratt. *In paper, price 1/-, by post 1/2.*

Pigeon-Keeping for Amateurs. A Complete Guide to the Amateur Breeder of Domestic and Fancy Pigeons. By J. C. Lyell. Illustrated. *In cloth gilt, with coloured plate, price 2/6, by post 2/9, in paper, price 1/, by post 1/2.*

Poker Work, A Guide to, including Coloured Poker Work and Relief Burning. A Practical Manual for Amateurs, containing a full Description of the necessary Tools, and Instructions for their use. By W. D. Thompson. Illustrated. *In paper, price 1/-, by post 1/2.*

Polishes and Stains for Woods : A Complete Guide to Polishing Woodwork, with Directions for Staining, and Full Information for Making the Stains, Polishes, &c., in the simplest and most satisfactory manner. By David Denning. *In paper, price 1/-, by post 1/2.*

Pool, Games of. Describing Various English and American Pool Games, and giving the Rules in full. Illustrated. *In paper, price 1/-, by post 1/2.*

Portraiture, Home, for Amateur Photographers. Being the result of many years' incessant work in the production of Portraits "at home." By P. R. Salmon (Richard Penlake), Editor of *The Photographic News*. Fully Illustrated. *In cloth gilt, price 2/6, by post 2/9.*

Postage Stamps, and their Collection. A Practical Handbook for Collectors of Postal Stamps, Envelopes, Wrappers, and Cards. By Oliver Firth, Member of the Philatelic Societies of London, Leeds, and Bradford. Profusely Illustrated. *In cloth gilt, price 2/6, by post 2/10.*

Postage Stamps of Europe, The Adhesive : A Practical Guide to their Collection, Identification, and Classification. Especially designed for the use of those commencing the Study. By W. A. S. Westoby. Beautifully Illustrated. Cheap and Revised Edition. *In 2 vols., cloth gilt, price 7/6, by post 8/-.*

In connection with these Publications on Postage Stamps we have arranged to supply Gauges for Measuring Perforations. These Stamp Gauges are made in brass, and can be carried in the waistcoat pocket. *Price 1/-, by post 1/1.*

Postmarks, History of British. With 350 Illustrations and a List of Numbers used in Obliterations. By J. H. Daniels. *In cloth gilt, price 2/6, by post 2/9.*

Postmarks of the British Isles, the History of the Early. From their Introduction down to 1840, with Special Remarks on and Reference to the Sections of the Postal Service to which they particularly applied. Compiled chiefly from Official Records by John G. Hendy, Curator of the Record Room, General Post Office. Illustrated. *In cloth, price 3/6, by post 3/9.*

Pottery and Porcelain, English. A Guide for Collectors. Handsomely Illustrated with Engravings of Specimen Pieces and the Marks used by the different Makers. With some account of the latest values realised. By the Rev. E. A. Downman. New Edition, Revised and Enlarged by Aubrey Gunn, Expert in old Pottery and Porcelain to *The Bazaar*. *In cloth gilt, price 6/-, by post 6/4.*

Poultry and Egg Raising at Home. A Practical Work, showing how Eggs and Poultry may be produced for Home Consumption with little expenditure of time or money. By W. M. Elkington. Illustrated. *In paper, price 1/-, by post 1/2.*

Poultry-Farming, Profitable. Describing in Detail the Methods that Give the Best Results, and pointing out the Mistakes to be Avoided. By J. H. Sutcliffe. Illustrated. *In paper, price 1/-, by post 1/2.*

Poultry for Prize and Profit. By Prof. J. Long. New Edition, Revised and Enlarged by W. M. Elkington. {In the press.

Poultry Incubators and their Management. By J. H. Sutcliffe. Fifth Edition, Revised. Illustrated. *In paper, price 1/-, by post 1/2.*

Poultry-Keeping, Popular. A Practical and Complete Guide to Breeding and Keeping Poultry for Eggs or for the Table. Second Edition, with Additional Matter and Illustrations. By W. M ELKINGTON. *In paper*, *price 1/, by post 1/2.*

Press Work for Women. A Practical Guide to the Beginner. What to Write, How to Write it, and Where to Send it. By FRANCES H LOW. *In paper, price 1/-, by post 1/2*

Rabbit, Book of the. A Complete Work on Breeding and Rearing all Varieties of Fancy Rabbits, giving their History, Variations, Uses, Points, Selection, Mating, Management, &c, &c. SECOND EDITION. Edited by KEMPSTER W. KNIGHT. Illustrated with Coloured and other Plates. *In cloth gilt, price 10/6, by post 10/11.*

Rabbits for Prizes and Profit. The Proper Management of Fancy Rabbits in Health and Disease, for Pets or the Market, and Descriptions of every known Variety, with Instructions for Breeding Good Specimens. By CHARLES RAYSON. Illustrated. *In cloth gilt, price 2/6, by post 2/9. Also in Sections, as follow.*

Rabbits, General Management of. Including Hutches, Breeding, Feeding, Diseases and their Treatment, Rabbit Courts, &c. Fully Illustrated. *In paper, price 1/-, by post 1/2*

Rabbits, Exhibition. Being descriptions of all Varieties of Fancy Rabbits, their Points of Excellence, and how to obtain them. Illustrated. *In paper, price 1/-, by post 1/2*

Repoussé Work for Amateurs. Being the Art of Ornamenting Thin Metal with Raised Figures. By L L. HASLOPE. Illustrated. *In paper, price 1/-, by post 1/2*

Roses for Amateurs. A Practical Guide to the Selection and Cultivation of the best Roses. Second Edition, with Sixteen Plates. By the REV. J HONY-WOOD D'OMBRAIN, Hon Sec. Nat Rose Soc. *In paper, price 1/-, by post 1/2*

Sailing Tours. The Yachtman's Guide to the Cruising Waters of the English and Adjacent Coasts. With Descriptions of every Creek, Harbour, and Road-stead on the Course. With numerous Charts printed in Colours, showing Deep water, Shoals, and Sands exposed at low water, with sounding. By FRANK COWPER, B A. *In crown 8vo, cloth gilt*

Vol I. The Coasts of Essex and Suffolk, from the Thames to Aldborough. Six Charts. *Price 5/-, by post 5/3.*
Vol. II. The South Coast, from the Thames to the Scilly Islands. Twenty-five Charts. New and Revised Edition. *Price 7/6, by post 7/10.* [Out of print
Vol. III. The Coast of Brittany, from L'Abervrach to St Nazaire, and an account of the Loire. Twelve Charts. *Price 7/6, by post 7/10*
Vol. IV. The West Coast, from Land's End to Mull of Galloway, including the East Coast of Ireland. Thirty Charts. *Price 10/6, by post 10/10*
Vol. V. The Coasts of Scotland and the N F of England down to Ald-borough. Forty Charts. *Price 10/6, by post 10/10*

St. Bernard Stud Book. Edited by HUGH DALZIEL. 2 Vols, containing Pedigrees of over 1800 Dogs up to 1891. *In cloth gilt, price 3/6 each, by post 3/9 each.*

Sea-Fishing for Amateurs. A Practical Book on Fishing from Shore, Rocks, or Piers, with a Directory of Fishing Stations on the English and Welsh Coasts. Illustrated by numerous Charts, showing the best spots for the various kinds of fish, position of rocks, &c. Second Edition, revised, enlarged, and copiously illustrated. By FRANK HUDSON. *In paper, price 1/-, by post 1/2*

Sea Fishing, Practical. A Comprehensive Handbook for all Sea Anglers, on the Best Tackle, and most Successful Methods of Sea Angling on our Coasts. By P L HASLOPE. Fully Illustrated. *In cloth, price 3/6, by post 3 9*

Sea-Life, Realities of. Describing the Duties, Prospects, and Pleasures of a Young Sailor in the Mercantile Marine. By H. E ACRAMAN COATE. With a Preface by J R. DIGGLE M A. *In cloth gilt, price 3/6, by post 3/10*

Seaside Watering Places. A description of the Holiday Resorts on the Coasts of England and Wales, the Channel and Scilly Islands, and the Isle of Man, giving full particulars of them and their attractions, and all information likely to assist persons in selecting places in which to spend their Holidays, according to their individual tastes. Profusely Illustrated   Thirtieth Year of Publication   *In one vol , cloth, price 2/6, by post 2/10.* Also in three Sections as under, *price 1/-, by post 1/2 ·* THE EAST COAST—From Spittal in Northumberland, to Littlestone-on-Sea, in Kent.   With 55 Illustrations. 100 Places to choose from.   THE SOUTH COAST—From Hastings in Sussex to Penzance, in Cornwall, including the Isle of Wight, Channel and Scilly Islands   57 Illustrations   85 Places to choose from.   THE WEST COAST—From St Ives in Cornwall, to Skinburness in Cumberland, including the Isle of Man.   66 Illustrations   129 Places to choose from.

Sea Terms, a Dictionary of. For the use of Yachtsmen, Voyagers, and all who go down to the sea in big or little ships   By A ANSTED. Fully Illustrated. *In cloth gilt, price 5/-, by post 5/4.*

Shadow Entertainments, and How to Work them · being Something about Shadows, and the way to make them Profitable and Funny.   By A, PATTERSON. Illustrated   *In paper, price 1/-, by post 1/2*

Sheet Metal, Working in: Being Practical Instructions for Making and Mending Small Articles in Tin, Copper, Iron, Zinc, and Brass.   By the Rev J LUKIN, B.A Illustrated   Third Edition   *In paper, price 1/-, by post 1/1*

Show Record, The. Being Part III of "The Breeders' and Exhibitors' Record," for the Registration of Particulars concerning the Exhibition of Pedigree stock of every Description By W K TAUNTON. *In cloth gilt, price 2/6, by post 2/9.*

Skating Cards: An Easy Method of Learning Figure Skating, as the Cards *can be used on the Ice   In cloth case, price 2/6, by post 2/9.* A cheap form is issued printed on paper and made up as a small book, *price 1/-, by post 1/1*

Sleight of Hand. A Practical Manual of Legerdemain for Amateurs and Others   New Edition, Revised and Enlarged. Illustrated. By E SACHS   *In cloth gilt, price 6/6, by post 6/10.*

Solo Whist. Its Whys and Wherefores   A Progressive and Clear Method of Explanation and Illustration of the Game, and how to Play it Successfully With Illustrative Hands printed in Colours   By C J MELROSE. *In cloth gilt, price 3/6, by post 3/10, in half leather, gilt top, price 5/6, by post 6/-*

Sporting Books, Illustrated. And their Values   Dealing with English Illustrated Works of a Sporting and Racy Character, and Prints relating to Sports of the Field   A very valuable book to all Owners or Collectors of old Sporting Books or Prints   Many a valuable old print has been thrown away for want of just such information as this book gives   By J H SLATER, Author of "Library Manual," "Engravings and Their Value," &c   *In cloth gilt, price 5/-, by post 5/4*

Stud Record, The. Being Part II of "The Breeders' and Exhibitors' Record," for the Registration of Particulars concerning Pedigree Stock of every Description. By W. K. TAUNTON. *In cloth gilt, price 2/6, by post 2/9.*

Swimming for Women and Girls. A Handbook of Practical Instruction By COLIN HAMILTON   With Special Chapters upon Costume and Training by a Lady Champion Swimmer. Fully illustrated by unique and specially taken Photographs. *In paper, price 1/-, by post 1/2.*

Taxidermy, Practical. A Manual of Instruction to the Amateur in Collecting, Preserving, and Setting-up Natural History Specimens of all kinds   With Examples and Working Diagrams   By MONTAGU BROWNE, F.Z S , Curator of Leicester Museum   Second Edition. *In cloth gilt, price 7/6, by post 7/10*

Tomato Culture for Amateurs. A Practical and very Complete Manual on the subject   By B C. RAVENSCROFT. New Edition   Illustrated   *In paper, price 1/ , by post 1/2*

Trapping, Practical : Being some Papers on Traps and Trapping for Vermin, with a Chapter on General Bird Trapping and Snaring   By W CARNEGIE Third Edition, Revised and Enlarged. *In paper, price 1/-, by post 1/2*

Tuning and Repairing Pianos. The Amateur's Guide to the Practical Management of a Cottage or Grand Piano without the intervention of a Professional. Third Edition, Revised and Enlarged   *In paper, price 1/-, by post 1/2*

Vamp, How to. A Practical Guide to the Accompaniment of Songs by the Unskilled Musician. With Examples *In paper, price 9d , by post 10d.*

Vegetable Culture for Amateurs. Containing Concise Directions for the Cultivation of Vegetables in small Gardens so as to insure Good Crops With Lists of the Best Varieties of each Sort. By W J. MAY. Illustrated *In paper, price 1/-, by post 1/2.*

Ventriloquism, Practical. A thoroughly reliable Guide to the Art of Voice Throwing and Vocal Mimicry, Vocal Instrumentation, Ventriloquial Figures, Entertaining, &c By ROBERT GANTHONY. Numerous Illustrations *In cloth gilt, price 2/-, by post 2/4.* Cheap Edition *In paper, price 1/-, by post 1/2.*

Violin School, Practical, for Home Students Instructions and Exercises in Violin Playing, for the use of Amateurs, Self-Learners, Teachers, and others. By J M FLEMING *In demy 4to, price 5/-, by post 5/6.*

Vivarium, The. Being a Full Description of the most Interesting Snakes Lizards, and other Reptiles, and How to Keep Them Satisfactorily in Confinement By REV G. C BATEMAN. Beautifully Illustrated. *In cloth gilt, price 7/6, by post 7/10*

Whippet or Race-Dog, The : How to Breed, Rear, Train, Race, and Exhibit the Whippet, the Management of Race Meetings, and Original Plans of Courses. By FREEMAN LLOYD. *In paper, price 1/ , by post 1/2.*

Whist, Solo : Its Whys and Wherefores. A Progressive and Clear Method of Explanation and Illustration of the Game, and how to Play it Successfully. With Illustrative Hands printed in Colours. By C. J. MELROSE. *In cloth gilt, price 3/6, by post 3/10 ; in half leather, gilt top, 5/6, by post 5/10.*

Whist, Scientific : Its Whys and Wherefores The Reader being taught by *Reason* rather than by arbitrary Rules With Illustrative Hands printed in Colours By C. J MELROSE *In cloth gilt, price 3/6, by post 3/10 ; in half leather, gilt top, 5/6, by post 5/10*

Wildfowling, Practical : A Book on Wildfowl and Wildfowl Shooting. New Edition By W T FALLON. *In cloth, price 6/ , by post 6/4.*

Wild Sports in Ireland. Being Picturesque and Entertaining Descriptions of several visits paid to Ireland, with Practical Hints likely to be of service to the Angler, Wildfowler, and Yachtsman By JOHN BICKERDIKE, Author of " The Book of the All-Round Angler," &c Beautifully illustrated from Photographs taken by the Author *In cloth gilt, price 6/-, by post 6/4.*

Window Ticket Writing. Containing full instructions on the Method of Mixing and using the Various Inks, &c., required, Hints on Stencilling as applied to Ticket Writing, together with Lessons on Glass Writing, Japanning on Tin, &c. Especially written for the use of Learners and Shop Assistants. By WM. C. SCOTT. *In paper, price 1/-, by post 1/2.*

Wire and Sheet Gauges of the World. Compared and Compiled by C. A. B PFEILSCHMIDT, of Sheffield *In paper, price 1/-, by post 1/1.*

Wood Carving for Amateurs. Full instructions for producing all the different varieties of Carvings SECOND EDITION Edited by D DENNING *In paper, price 1/-, by post 1/2*

Workshop Makeshifts. Being a Collection of Practical Hints and Suggestions for the use of Amateur Workers in Wood and Metal. By H J. S. CASSAL. Fully Illustrated *In cloth gilt, price 2/6, by post 2/9.*

Wrestling. A Practical Handbook upon the Catch hold and Græco-Roman Styles of Wrestling , a splendid system of Athletic Training. By PERCY LONGHURST, winner in the Light-weight Competition, G G S , 1899 Author of " Jiu-Jitsu and other Methods of Self-Defence " Profusely Illustrated. *In paper, price 1/-, by post 1/2*

Wrestling. *See* " Jiu-Jitsu," page 10.

All Books are Nett.

CPSIA information can be obtained
at www.ICGtesting.com
Printed in the USA
LVHW020208130423
744269LV00009B/157